Tugs in Colour - British Built

by

Andrew Wiltshire

In the late 1960s Shell's Tranmere terminal on Merseyside was destined to receive larger vessels, and this brought with it the requirement for more powerful tugs which would have to possess a fire-fighting capability. For this contract the Rea Towing Co Ltd of Liverpool provided a pair of impressive vessels, the **Brackengarth** and **Hollygarth**. Completed in 1969 by Appledore Shipbuilders Ltd, these tugs had a bollard pull of 50 tonnes. They were each powered by a pair of English Electric diesels developing 3380bhp, which were geared to drive a single controllable pitch propeller. In 1985 ownership passed to Cory Towage Ltd and the following year

the **Brackengarth** transferred to Irish Tugs Ltd, eventually being registered at Westport under the Irish flag. Now regularly employed on coastal towing duties, it is in this period that we see her at Barry in dramatic lighting on 2 September 1989. In 1995 she was sold to Finnish owner Reino Henriksson Oy of Pori as **Henric**. Her subsequent history was extensive with numerous changes of owner. She was known to still be in service in 2016 as the Norwegian-owned **Stone** of Miljostein Shipping A/S, Hvalstad.

(the late John Wiltshire)

INTRODUCTION

This book is intended as a sequel to my first book on tugs *Looking Back at British Tugs* (2007), and this time concentrates on examples that were completed in British shipyards. I have always been fascinated by the number of small shipyards that once existed around the UK, and often by the location of these yards. Many of them specialised in building tugs large and small for the home market as well as for customers overseas, and not just in the British colonies. Such was the quality of British-built tugs, that some went on to give many years of service. In 2016 a surprising number that have exceeded their 50th birthday can be found hard at work at locations around the world. It is a matter for regret that nearly all of these shipyards are now no more than a distant memory, and in the last twenty years, only a handful of tugs have been completed in the UK. This book covers tugs built at no fewer than 46 different shipyards, and I apologise if I have not been able to include a tug from a yard that the reader may have been particularly interested in.

Some abbreviations used throughout are: grt (gross registered tonnage), bhp (brake horse power) and ihp (indicated horsepower).

Acknowledgements

Many thanks must go to Paul Boot, Trevor Jones, Alastair Paterson and Simon Smith for their efforts in getting the project started. A big thank you must also go out to all the other contributors including Danny Lynch and René Beauchamp for the time and effort they have willingly given to my requests for help. Pete Brabham has very kindly given his time and skills to digitally renovate a number of the images in the book. I am very grateful to Bernard McCall for supporting this project and Gil Mayes for checking the captions; and of course my wife Tracey, for her encouragement throughout. Once again, I thank all the staff of Amadeus Press for their hard work in producing a fine finished volume. Lastly I must not forget my friends at the Barry Model Boat Club for their interest in my publications. I would like to dedicate this book to my late father John Wiltshire who introduced me to ships and the sea.

References used throughout include copies of Ian Allan *Coastal Ships*, *Lekko* and *Ships Monthly* magazines, *Lloyds Register* publications, *Seahorses of the Tees* and *150 Years of the Maltese Cross* (both by John H Proud), *Fifty Years of Naval Tugs* (by Bill Hannan), *Blow Five* (by W B Hallam), *Thames Ship Towage 1933-1992* (by John Reynolds), *A Century of South African Steam Tugs* (by David Reynolds), *Red Funnel and Before* (by R B Adams), *The Clyde Shipping Company Glasgow* (by Harvey and Telford) plus the World Ship Society publications *Empire Tugs* and *Cory Towage Ltd*.

Andrew Wiltshire   Cardiff   July 2016

Published by Bernard McCall, 400 Nore Road, Portishead, Bristol, BS20 8EZ, England.
Website : www.coastalshipping.co.uk.   Telephone/fax : 01275 846178.   Email : bernard@coastalshipping.co.uk.
All distribution enquiries should be addressed to the publisher.
Printed by The Amadeus Press, Ezra House, 26 West Business Park, Cleckheaton, BD19 4TQ.
Telephone : 01274 863210.   Fax: 01274 863211.   Email: info@amadeuspress.co.uk;   Website : www.amadeuspress.co.uk.
ISBN : 978-1-902953-80-9

Front cover : Shipbuilder J I Thornycroft & Company Limited was founded in 1866 at Chiswick, but later moved to a larger yard on the River Itchen at Woolston in Southampton. Here they built up a reputation for completing naval craft, but also constructed small numbers of ferries and tugs. The Southampton, Isle of Wight and South of England Royal Mail Steam Packet Co Ltd turned to this yard in 1923 for a twin-screw steam tug which was delivered as **Canute**. The **Thorness** was the fifth motor tug from Thornycroft when delivered on 28 March 1961, and was a very similar vessel to the **Dunnose** of 1958. At 247 tons gross she was a twin-screw tug powered by a pair of Crossley HGN-type diesels with a combined output of 1400bhp. This view of the **Thorness** was taken on 14 May 1983, during her last few months of service at Southampton. Later that year she crossed the Atlantic to join the Canadian fleet of J D Irving Ltd, St John, New Brunswick, as **Irving Juniper**. She later became **Atlantic Juniper** and was re-engined with a pair of Caterpillar diesels. By 2013 she was reported to be laid up out of use on the Saint John River.

(the late John Wiltshire)

Rear cover : Vokins & Co Ltd operated a small fleet of lighterage and launch tugs on the River Thames, and in particular in and around the West India Docks, the Royal Docks and on the River Lea. In 1937 Vokins took delivery of the small motor tug **Vanoc** which was followed in 1940 by the **Vista**. Both were completed by Richard Dunston, Thorne, and the **Vanoc** had a gross tonnage of 58 and an overall length of 68 feet. When built she had an open wheelhouse and a much taller funnel than we see in this view of her taken in October 1970. She is seen entering the River Thames having left the Royal Docks. In the background and of interest are the **Napia**, **Fossa**, **Sun XXIII** and **Sun III** of London Tugs Ltd. In 1975 **Vanoc** passed to Thames & General Lighterage Co Ltd, Greenwich, as **General I**. In 1983 she was renamed **Warrior** after being sold to Ron Livett, Greenwich. It is thought that in the late 1980s the former **Vanoc** lost her original 390bhp diesel and in its place gained a more powerful 860bhp power unit. By 2006 she was in poor condition and despite attempts to renovate her for further use, she was broken up near Pipers Wharf, Greenwich in 2013.

(the late C C Beazley)

In December 1966 the Alexandra Towing Co Ltd obtained control of Liverpool Screw Towing Co Ltd and its subsidiary North West Tugs Ltd, and collectively known as "Cock Tugs". With this came seven steam and five motor vessels. The steam tugs, two of which gained Alexandra names and livery in 1970, were sold between 1967 and 1971. The motor tugs also received traditional Alexandra names and one of these is the *Gladstone* which dates from 1960. She is seen near Eastham in July 1972 and looks particularly smart in Alexandra colours. She was previously Liverpool Screw Towing's *Flying Cock*

having been completed at Birkenhead by Cammell Laird & Co (Shipbuilders & Engineers) Ltd. The five motor tugs were sold to Greek owner N E Vernicos in 1981, but three were wrecked on the west Wales coast later that year, never reaching Greece. The *Gladstone* was one of the pair that did make it to Greek waters under the name *Vernicos Martin*, and from 1994 as *Agios Andreas* she continued to give good service until at least 2004. She was later reported as being broken up at Aliaga, Turkey during 2011.

(Paul Boot)

The large steam-powered twin-screw harbour tugs constructed for the South African Railways were all products of British shipyards. They were without doubt very handsome ships and attracted the attention of many ship lovers around the world. Ferguson Bros (Port Glasgow) Ltd were responsible for five of these from their yard at Port Glasgow, including the final example built, *J R More* of 1961. The *A M Campbell* and her sister *F T Bates* were completed in 1951 and featured an improved design of hull and superstructure, and were regarded as extended-range vessels with both fire-fighting and salvage capability. The *A M Campbell* is the subject of our image and makes a fine sight here arriving at Cape Town, in what is probably 1977. She was delivered to the Union Government of South Africa (Railways & Harbours Administration) in April 1951 and was initially based at Durban. She had a gross tonnage of 787 tons and an overall length of 175 feet. Both *A M Campbell* and *F T Bates* had oil-fired boilers and each tug was powered by a pair of Ferguson Bros-built triple expansion steam engines. The *A M Campbell* was transferred to Cape Town in 1968, eventually seeing out her days at Walvis Bay. She was withdrawn from service in September 1982 and sold to Underwater Construction & Salvage Co Pty Ltd, and was recorded as broken up at Walvis Bay by January 1984.

(the late Ken White)

In 1967 two virtually identical motor tugs entered service on the River Tyne for Lawson-Batey Tugs Ltd of Newcastle. They were **Northsider** in April, followed by **Ironsider** in September. Both were completed on north Humberside by Richard Dunston (Hessle) Ltd of Hessle, and had an overall length of 99 feet. The earlier **Westsider** of 1964 had featured a 6-cylinder Klöckner-Humboldt-Deutz diesel which must have made an impression as **Northsider** and **Ironsider** were installed with a larger 8-cylinder version developing 1420bhp which gave the pair a useful bollard pull of 18½ tonnes. In this view dated 15 August 1981 the **Ironsider** is seen heading upstream past North Shields. In 1986 she was chartered to Tyne Tugs Ltd and later carried Lawson Batey's buff funnel colour featuring a blue Maltese cross. In 1992 she was sold to Proodos Naftiki Eteria (Megalohari Hellenic Tugboats), of Piraeus, becoming **Megalochari XII**. By 2008 she was with Tugs Hatzigabriel Shipping Co. also of Piraeus, and bearing the name **Asteri**.

(the late Les Ring)

Until the mid-1950s, ship towage on the Clyde was still in the hands of steam tugs, but this was all about to change. Steel & Bennie Ltd of Glasgow purchased their first new motor tugs in 1957 and undertook to convert the steam tugs **Chieftain** and **Warrior** to motor in 1958. The **Chieftain** was sold in 1967 and a new motor tug bearing this name was delivered the following year. She was built by Scott and Sons (Bowling) Ltd. The new **Chieftain** was powered by an 8-cylinder Klöckner-Humboldt-Deutz diesel of 1650bhp, and had a steerable Kort nozzle which gave the tug a bollard pull of 27 tonnes. In 1970 Steel & Bennie Ltd were taken over by Cory Ship Towage (Clyde) Ltd, which in 1985 was restyled as Cory Towage Ltd. It is after this that we see the **Chieftain** underway on the Clyde, and in the later Cory livery which suits the tug well. She was sold by Cory in 1996 to Rod Jenkins Marine of Poole, gaining the name **Chief R** the following year. In March 1998 she was sold to United Arab Emirates interests as **Warm Seas IV** and working for Warm Seas Development & Trading L.L.C., registered in Sharjah. Ultimately the former **Chieftain** was broken up at Alang in India during 2005.

(Danny Lynch)

During the latter part of 1962, Newport Screw Towing Co Ltd took delivery of their first motor tugs, **Duncurlew** and **Dunsnipe**. Both were completed by Richard Dunston at Hessle and were single-screw vessels of 186grt with an overall length of 101 feet. The main engine was a 2-stroke British Polar diesel of 1260bhp making them the most powerful tugs in south-east Wales at the time. A similar vessel, **Dunosprey**, joined the fleet in 1968, but this featured an improved wheelhouse design as well as bridge control of the main engine. The Newport Screw Towing business passed to R & J H Rea Ltd in 1970, which was absorbed into Cory Ship Towage Ltd the following year. The

Duncurlew became **Westgarth** and gained Cory colours as depicted in this view of her off Newport, and looking a little the worse for wear on 21 August 1976. In 1981 she was sold to A Enebakk A/S at Lodingen in Norway and renamed **Nordbever**. She was subsequently re-engined in 1989 with a 7-cylinder Wichmann of 1750bhp, while her appearance changed drastically having received a new wheelhouse and funnel. In 2014 she is still at work in Norwegian waters as **Geitung** of J K Haaland, Haugesund.

(Nigel Jones)

The **Napia** was one of the last working steam tugs on the Thames and was completed as a Modified Warrior or Roach class Empire tug. She was delivered to the Ministry of War Transport in July 1943 as *Empire Jester* having been built by Goole Shipbuilding & Repairing Co Ltd. This builder was based on the Dutch River at Goole and had occupied this yard since 1917. Many coasters, trawlers and tugs were built, some for overseas customers, prior to the yard closing in the 1980s. On 14 May 1946 the *Empire Jester* passed to William Watkins Ltd, London, and was renamed *Napia*. Ship Towage (London) Ltd were appointed managers in February 1950. She had a grt of 261 and was powered by a 1000ihp triple expansion steam engine by McKie and Baxter Ltd and was converted to an oil-fired vessel in May 1950. In 1968 her owners were restyled as London Tugs Ltd after amalgamation with W H J Alexander Ltd and it is in London Tugs colours that we see her off Gravesend in 1971. Shortly afterwards, she was withdrawn from service passing to Greek owner J G Efthimou for further service at Piraeus as *Tolmiros*. In 1973 she was sold to Loucas G Matsas, also at Piraeus, and was eventually demolished at Perama during 1986.

(the late C C Beazley)

The **Tregeagle** was one of a small number of tugs completed by John Lewis & Sons Ltd at Aberdeen during the 1960s. In business as shipbuilders from 1907 until 1976, Lewis usually specialised in cargo ships and trawlers. The **Tregeagle** had been owned by Fowey Harbour Commissioners since 1986, and is seen underway in Fowey harbour in April 1989. At Fowey she was one of two similar sized tugs that could be called upon to assist larger vessels in the port. Prior to her service at Fowey she was the **Forth** of Forth Tugs Ltd at Grangemouth who purchased her from Clyde Shipping Co. Ltd, Glasgow, in 1984. With Clyde Shipping she was named **Flying Demon** having been delivered in April 1964. Her main engine was a 6-cylinder 2-stroke British Polar diesel developing 1000bhp, driving a controllable pitch propeller in a steerable Kort nozzle. Her duties at Fowey were considered to be over in 2008 when she was sold, eventually passing on 28 February 2013 to McCormick Transport. She was registered to its subsidiary company Foyle and Marine Dredging Co Ltd, Londonderry.

(Bernard McCall)

The **Mickry** was one of two elderly steam tugs still in use with the Leith Dock Commissioners at Leith in the 1960s, the other tug being the larger **Oxcar** of 1919. Both were sold for scrap locally in 1967, having been replaced by the new Voith Schneider tractor tugs **Gunnet** and **Inchcolm**. Built in the Netherlands, the **Oxcar** had arrived at Leith as long ago as 1925, whereas **Mickry** was acquired in 1946. At that time towage in the port was provided by Leith Salvage & Towage Co Ltd, and **Mickry** was obtained from Steel & Bennie Ltd at Glasgow, in whose fleet she had been named **Vanguard**. She had been completed in June 1920 by Bow, McLachlan & Co Ltd, whose yard was on the Clyde at Thistle Works, Paisley. She had a gross tonnage of 172 and was powered by a triple expansion engine of 750ihp. Bow, McLachlan & Co Ltd built numerous tugs over the years, but the yard stopped building ships in 1932. In 1953 Leith Salvage & Towage Co Ltd became the Leith Dock Commissioners and went on to purchase two motor tugs in 1958.

(Alastair Paterson)

C H Bailey Ltd was engaged in ship repairing and dry dock operations, initially in South Wales, but later managed Malta Dockyard on behalf of the Government of Malta. The company formed Atlantic Shipbuilding Co in 1953, based on the River Usk in Newport, and among the vessels completed were a pair of motor tugs in 1961 for its Malta operations. The tugs were named **Chris B.** and **Sara B.** and were delivered to C H Bailey Ltd at Valletta in August and October 1961 respectively. They were of 140 gross tons. In 1967 they passed to Midmed Towage Co Ltd of Valletta and the **Sara B.** became **St Lucian**. Midmed Towage was merged into Tug Malta Ltd in 1981 and another name change to **Gerit** took place. From 1982 the former **Sara B.** passed through the hands of a number of Greek owners, spending several years at Rhodes as **Herakles**. We see her at Rhodes on 19 September 1990. In 2004 her name was modified to **Heraclis** and in 2016 was thought to be still in service. The Atlantic Shipbuilding yard closed in 1970.

(Nigel Jones)

The second post-war motor tug for C J King & Sons (Tugs) Ltd of Bristol was the **Sea Volunteer** of 1963. She was constructed at the yard of W J Yarwood & Sons Ltd, Northwich, and was delivered to the Bristolian Steam Tug Co Ltd in March 1963 for use at Avonmouth, and was managed by C J King & Sons. She was a sister to **Sea Merrimac** built at Bristol in 1964. This view of **Sea Volunteer** dates from 18 May 1975 by which time her owner was given as C J King & Sons (Tugs) Ltd of Bristol. The C J King fleet was merged with Cory Ship Towage Ltd in February 1983 to form Cory King Towage, but the two vessels mentioned above were not included in the deal. Along with **Sea Merrimac**, the **Sea Volunteer** passed to Pounds Shipowners and Shipbreakers Ltd, Brockenhurst, and was resold in 1985 to Atlantic Tug & Shipping Ltd, becoming **Wrestler** and **Pullman** under the Panamanian flag. By 1987 the former **Sea Volunteer** had passed to a Maltese owner for conversion into a fishing vessel. As such she sank in the Atlantic during a storm, and bearing the name **Immanuel II**.

(Nigel Jones)

It is always good to see a new photograph of a steam tug in action, and this view is particularly special as it depicts a fine-looking British-built example at work in a port that rarely appears in images. The **Cochin** dated from 1933 and was completed by Henry Robb Ltd, Leith, . She was launched on 14 February 1933 and delivered shortly after to the Indian Government (Province of Madras) for use at Cochin, a port on the west coast of India. She was completed with a gross tonnage of 273, and at 110 feet in length was classed as a salvage tug. The **Cochin** was powered by a pair of triple expansion steam engines manufactured by Plenty & Son Ltd, and delivering a combined output of 1000ihp. Her boilers were oil-fired, and on trials she attained her design speed of 12 knots. In this view at Cochin, she is running alongside the Indian-flag freighter **Indian Industry** of 1959. The tug was still recorded as being in existence with the Government of the Republic of India in 1986, but her ultimate fate is unknown.

(Stan Tedford)

The Grangemouth & Forth Towing Co. Ltd operated at least ten paddle tugs at Grangemouth and Methil between 1895 and 1966. The **Roker** was one of a pair of steel-hulled paddle tugs delivered to Sunderland Towing Co. (J E Dawson) of Sunderland in early 1905, her sister being the **Whitburn**. The pair were completed by J P Rennoldson & Sons at South Shields, and each had gross tonnage of 119. Power was obtained from a 350ihp 2-cylinder side-lever steam engine and they had a speed of 10 knots. In 1913 the **Whitburn** passed to The Grangemouth & Forth Towing Co Ltd which, apart from a break for war service between 1940 and 1945, kept her running until 1958. The **Roker** on the other hand passed into the ownership of France, Fenwick, Tyne & Wear Co Ltd, Sunderland, in 1918 and remained based on the River Wear until 1962. By coincidence, she then joined the Grangemouth & Forth Towing fleet, albeit four years after the demise of her sistership. She was modified slightly to make her more suitable for use in exposed conditions, and was put to work at Methil harbour in Fife, where she replaced the **Elie** of 1912. This view shows the **Roker** at work at Methil in September 1963, and she appears to be devoid of any life-saving apparatus. Her career came to an end in March 1966 when she was sold for breaking up at St Davids harbour on the Forth.

(Alastair Paterson)

Early motor tugs to appear on the River Tyne were a series of five vessels completed by the North Devon shipyard of P K Harris & Sons Ltd at Appledore. They were delivered to France, Fenwick, Tyne & Wear Co. Ltd in 1955/56 and were named **Alnwick**, **Ashbrooke**, **Bamburgh**, **Marsden** and **Prestwick**. Rather unusually all were fitted with second-hand 12-cylinder General Motors diesel engines of about 1080bhp. The **Ashbrooke** and **Bamburgh** had been withdrawn from service by early 1981, and in this view they are seen laid up in the South Dock at Sunderland on 1 June 1981. Both were sold to Greek owners in 1982 and they were given the names **Anikitos** and **Karapiperis III** respectively, but the deals did not proceed and both tugs reverted to their original names and remained laid up and under arrest at Sunderland in 1983. It is thought that both the **Ashbrooke** and **Bamburgh** departed for service in Greek waters by 1986, with **Bamburgh** eventually assuming the name **Sostis** and registered in Piraeus.

(the late Les Ring)

J Samuel White & Co. Ltd. commenced shipbuilding at East Cowes in the 1880s, completing vessels such as torpedo boats, yachts and paddle steamers. After WWII they returned to completing merchant ships including ferries, refrigerated fruit ships and a number of tugs, and the yard closed to shipbuilding in 1964. J P Knight of Rochester on the Medway took delivery of the motor tug **Kestrel** from this Isle of Wight shipyard in 1955. She had a grt of 223, an overall length of 102 feet, and was powered by an 8-cylinder British Polar diesel of 1150bhp. A similar but slightly larger tug named **Kenley** appeared with J P Knight three years later, but had been built on the Clyde by Lobnitz and Co Ltd at Renfrew. Both **Kestrel** and **Kenley** were transferred to Invergordon in the early 1970s to work for associated Caledonian Towage Co Ltd, and remained there until withdrawn from service in late 1983. They were then sold to a shipbreaker at Milton Creek near Sittingbourne. This view of **Kestrel** was taken at Peterhead in October 1978, with the ruins of Old St Peter's church in the background.

(Alastair Paterson)

Liverpool-based Johnston Warren Lines Ltd, part of the Furness, Withy group of companies, had three steam tugs in operation at that port in the 1950s and these were replaced by three motor tugs in 1958. The **Foylemore** and **Kilmore**, constructed by W J Yarwood & Sons Ltd at Northwich, followed the Bristol-built **Rossmore**. In 1968 Furness, Withy indicated their desire to withdraw from towing activities and the three tugs above passed to Rea Towing Co Ltd, becoming **Rossgarth**, **Foylegarth** and **Kilgarth** in 1969. This view of an immaculate **Foylegarth** out on the River Mersey dates from the autumn of 1979. The **Foylegarth** was sold in March 1983 to Pounds Shipowners and Shipbreakers Ltd and sold on two months later to Falmouth Towage Co Ltd as **St Budoc** and she put in a further 19 years' service. She later passed to Western Marine Salvage Ltd, Holy Loch, where it is thought that she remained inactive although the intention was that she would tow barges laden with round timber. She sailed for Portland, Dorset, in 2008 to be prepared for delivery to African owners. However sale was not concluded and in 2010 the tug, still bearing the name **St Budoc**, arrived at New Holland for breaking up.

(Laurie Schofield)

The last steam tugs to be constructed for Alexandra Towing Co Ltd were a series of ten similar vessels delivered from a number of different yards between 1954 and 1959. Three were added to the fleet in 1954, coming from Cochrane & Sons Ltd at Selby; and named **Waterloo**, **Wallasey** and **Canning**. The **Canning** was built as an oil-fired tug as were the subsequent seven tugs which commenced with the **North Light** in January 1956 and concluded with the **North Wall** in August 1959. This photograph of the **Waterloo** was taken at Swansea on 28 January 1969. The old breakwater in the background would soon be demolished. The **Waterloo** had been a

Swansea-based tug for a number of years when she returned to Liverpool in 1962 for her boiler to be converted from coal to oil-burning. Upon return to Swansea she continued to work alongside **Wallasey** and was joined by the **Canning** from Liverpool in 1966. The **Waterloo** was withdrawn from service in 1972 and sold to Italian owner Società Rimorchiatori Napoletani who repainted her in their house colours with the name **Dritto**, before sailing for a new working life at Naples. It was not until 1988 that she was taken out of service and eventually broken up at Naples during 1989.

(the late John Wiltshire)

Two large motors tugs were completed by Cochrane & Sons Ltd, Selby for service on the lower Thames and in particular the oil terminals at Isle of Grain and Shell Haven. For this role they were built with a substantial mast-mounted fire-fighting platform featuring four monitors, which gave the pair an unmistakable outline. The first tug was the *Avenger* delivered in November 1962 to the Elliott Steam Tug Co (1949) Ltd, followed in January 1963 by the *Hibernia* for William Watkins Ltd. The *Hibernia* had a gross tonnage of 293 and an overall length of 118 feet and her main engine was a British Polar 2-stroke diesel of 1800bhp. She was taken into the London Tugs Ltd fleet in 1968 and in 1974 was upgraded with a controllable pitch propeller and a Kort nozzle. London Tugs Ltd was taken over in 1975 by Alexandra Towing Co Ltd. The *Avenger* passed to Greek owners at Thessaloniki in 1987 as *Atrotos*, and by 1991 was sailing as *Karapiperis X*, a name later modified to *Karapiperis 10*. This photograph dates from 29 October 2006 and depicts her as the *Alfios* and operated by Katakolon Tugboat Services Shipping Co, of Katakolon. Still bearing the name *Alfios*, she passed to Ergasies Rimoulkiseos Katakolou Naftiki Eteria, Piraeus, by 2011, and was still in service in 2015.

(Paul Boot)

The first new motor tugs for Alexandra Towing Co Ltd. of Liverpool were the **North Isle** and **North Loch** of 1959, which spent most of their time with Alexandra, based at Southampton. They had been completed by W J Yarwood & Sons, Northwich, to whom Alexandra returned for another pair of motor tugs destined for use at Swansea and Port Talbot. Delivered in July and October 1961 as **Gower** and **Talbot**, they were attractive-looking tugs, with innovative features such as a controllable pitch propeller installed in a Kort nozzle. They had a gross tonnage of 152 and were powered by an 8-cylinder Crossley Bros oil engine developing 865bhp. For over twenty years they were based at

Swansea and also serviced Port Talbot docks and later the new tidal harbour. This superb image of the **Gower** passing the new breakwater was taken at Swansea on 7 June 1973, the tug having just left the lock. The **Talbot** was sold to Greek owners in 1984 becoming **Achilleas** and was still at work at Volos in 2015. The **Gower** on the other hand was sold to Benfleet Solutions Ltd in 1985 and, having passed to Greek owners in February 1986, was renamed **Kostas** in 1986, and was last heard of in Greek waters in about 2006.

(the late John Wiltshire)

We now look at tugs built by Charles Hill in Bristol. Charles Hill & Sons Ltd was established in 1845 and went out of business in 1977. The Union Government of South Africa (Railways & Harbours Administration) operated some fine-looking steam tugs and Charles Hill produced one example in 1950, the *J D White*, which was named after Brigadier John Dunbar White, an advisor to the South African Ministry of Transport. She was a large tug at 642 gross tons and had an overall length of 161 feet. She was twin-screw and featured a pair of triple expansion steam engines manufactured by Plenty & Son Ltd of Newbury

with a combined output of 3200ihp. On builders trials she reached a speed of just over 12 knots. The *J D White* began her career based at Durban but moved on to Walvis Bay before spending her final years at East London, which is where we see her in this rather splendid view. She was withdrawn from service on 25 September 1980, the last coal-burning steam tug in service in South Africa. She was broken up in August 1981 at East London.

(the late Pernell Mizen, courtesy Trevor Jones collection)

Following the entry into service of two modern motor tugs, **Avongarth** and **Plumgarth** at Avonmouth in 1960 (see page 42), R & J H Rea Ltd placed an order for a further pair for 1962 delivery. They were of a similar size, but this time would be from the local shipyard of Charles Hill & Sons Ltd in Bristol. The first to be delivered in April 1962 was **Polgarth** followed in September by **Pengarth**. As before they featured a Ruston & Hornsby engine, but this time a more powerful 6-cylinder version with an output of 1080bhp. It was quite common for one of this pair to sail to Cardiff to help out when shipping movements were busy, but on this occasion the **Pengarth** is working at Avonmouth. The date is 20 April 1976, and she is being deployed as the bow tug on T & J Harrison's general cargo vessel **Benefactor**. The **Pengarth** had been in the colours of Cory Ship Towage Ltd since 1970, and in 1985 these changed again to those of Cory Towage Ltd, which were not too dissimilar to the livery worn in her R & J H Rea days. She was sold in 1991 to Peninsular Shipping Co Ltd, St Peter Port, Guernsey, but soon resold to Survey & Supply Ltd, at Grimsby. After a five year spell with Tyne Towage, Newcastle, the **Pengarth** was sold in 1997 to Togo Oil and Marine for service in West Africa. She underwent her first change of name at this stage to **Vigilant**; her continued existence was however in doubt after 2005.

(Andrew Wiltshire)

18

F A Ashmead & Sons was a tug and barge owner from Bristol, who amongst other things was originally engaged with bringing barges carrying tobacco from Avonmouth to the City Docks at Bristol. In 1959 Ashmead purchased the small tug **Volunteer** from C J King and named her **Robert A**. In 1970 he acquired King's other early motor tug, **John King**. The **John King** had been launched in 1935 by Charles Hill & Sons Ltd and delivered in February 1936 to the Alarm Steam Tug Co. Ltd. (C J King & Sons Ltd) primarily for use in the City Docks and River Avon. She was originally powered by a 4-cylinder Petter diesel of 300bhp, but this was replaced in 1962 by a 6-cylinder Lister Blackstone of 337bhp. Ashmead renamed her **Peter Leigh** and until her sale

in 1976 she was employed towing barges carrying hard wood logs for furniture manufacture to Lydney dock from Avonmouth, until her sale in 1976. Here she is seen underway in Avonmouth docks on 1 September 1971. She saw further service with new owners initially as **Pride** and from 1992 as **Durdham**. She was acquired in 1994 by the Bristol Industrial Museum for preservation, and soon regained her original name **John King**. Her restoration was completed in 2000 and in 2016 she was still in use with the M Shed museum, occasionally running passenger trips around Bristol Harbourside.

(the late John Wiltshire)

By far the largest tugs completed at Bristol by Charles Hill & Sons Ltd were a pair of deep-sea salvage tugs for the Polish Government in the late 1950s. The first completed was the **Jantar** which was delivered in November 1958 to Polskie Ratownictwo Okretowe at Gdynia. Her sister was launched as **Eol** but completed for the same owner as **Koral** in June 1959. They had a gross tonnage of 1281 and were 215 feet in length and 40 feet in the beam. Two main engines were installed, these being 7-cylinder four-stroke diesels by National Gas & Oil Engine Company with a combined output of 3150bhp, and geared to a single propeller shaft. They had a service speed of 15½ knots and the hull was constructed for operation in ice. The **Koral** is seen on the New Waterway on 21 September 1975, and was a common sight in northern European waters, although she did venture much further afield. By 1981 her owner was described as Polish Ship Salvage Co. and in 1989 she passed to German owners as **Ora**, and was immediately resold to Indian shipbreakers at Alang. Her sister **Jantar** remained under the Polish flag until the end, and passed to breakers in Pakistan in 1992.

(the late C C Beazley collection)

After the closure of Charles Hill's shipyard in 1976, the site was once again used for shipbuilding and repairs from 1980, when David Abels Boatbuilders Ltd set up business here. Early completions were the small 170bhp tugs **Maria McLoughlin** and **Sarah McLoughlin** of 1981. In 1997 a much larger tug of 120grt was completed for Maritime Craft Services (Clyde) Ltd, a company founded in 1977 to provide support for construction and dredging contracts. Named **MCS Lenie**, she was a twin-screw vessel with a length of 24,35m and beam of 8,83m and an open stern. She was powered by a pair of Caterpillar diesels delivering 2200bhp, which gave her a bollard pull of 26 tonnes and a speed of 11 knots. We see her at Newport having just delivered the former Isle of Wight passenger ferry **Southsea** from Bristol, for continued lay-up. The **MCS Lenie** was later fitted with a bow-thruster unit and went on charter to the Ministry of Defence for use at Kyle of Lochalsh. In 2008 she was purchased by Serco Denholm Marine Services Ltd and renamed **SD Kyle of Lochalsh** for continued use on the west coast of Scotland.

(Danny Lynch)

The **Cabot** was a small twin-screw tug and a familiar sight in Avonmouth and the Bristol City Docks for over twenty years. She featured a passenger saloon and was occasionally used for port inspection tours as well as towing duties with dredging plant and a grain elevator. Her licence for 45 passengers enabled her to be used to host civil dignitaries such as the Lord Mayor and Port Authority officers. The **Cabot** was completed in 1952 at Bristol by Charles Hill & Sons Ltd and delivered to The Lord Mayor Aldermen and Burgesses of the City of Bristol in June that year. Her name commemorates Italian mariner and explorer John Cabot who discovered North America in 1497, and in whose memory the Cabot Tower in Bristol was built. The tug had an overall length of 80 feet and was powered by a pair of 3-cylinder British Polar diesels. In 1963 her owners became Port of Bristol Authority and the same year she had her engines replaced with a pair of 8-cylinder Gardner diesels. The **Cabot** was sold in 1974 to McCann Tugs Ltd of London, and she is noted here at Whitehaven in August 1975. She was later chartered to Winnie Towing Co, Lowestoft in 1982. Her latter years were spent in Ireland and she was eventually broken up in 1995 at Oldcourt in County Cork, having never changed her name.

(the late John Wiltshire collection)

We now look at some tugs built at Hessle on the north bank of the Humber where there was a history of shipbuilding dating back to the late 17th century. In 1897 Henry Scarr set up a yard at Hessle Haven which was acquired by Richard Dunston Ltd of Thorne in 1932. The Hessle yard continued to trade under the title Henry Scarr Ltd until 1961. At the time she was completed in March 1955, the **Vanquisher** was the most powerful single-screw tug in service on the River Thames. She had a gross tonnage of 294 and was a very distinctive tug. She was delivered from Henry Scarr to the Elliott Steam Tug Co (1949) Ltd, and later was classed as a tug/tender, having a certificate to carry 100 passengers. The **Vanquisher** was powered by an 8-cylinder British Polar diesel of 1280bhp giving her a speed of 12 knots. In 1965 her ownership transferred to William Watkins Ltd and then to the newly-formed London Tugs Ltd in 1969. This is how we see her in 1970 in an entrance lock to the Royal docks. Alexandra Towing Co Ltd of Liverpool took control of London Tugs in 1975. On 8 January 1976, whilst undocking container ship **Jervis Bay** from Tilbury, the **Vanquisher** was girted and sank. She was quickly raised and put back into service. In June 1982 she was sold for breaking up at Bloors Wharf, Rainham.

(the late C C Beazley)

The Alexandra Towing Co Ltd owned three Empire-type steam tugs and two of these were from the Birch Class design being completed by Henry Scarr Ltd for the Ministry of War Transport. These were the **Brambles** of 1942, formerly **Empire Teak**, and **Flying Kestrel** of 1943 which was completed as **Empire Mascot**. Both tugs formed part of the Southampton fleet before ending their days working at Swansea. The **Flying Kestrel** had in fact been acquired from Metal Industries Ltd, Glasgow, in 1948 with whom she had spent a year or so as **Metinda IV**. She had a gross tonnage of 244 and was powered by a 1000ihp triple expansion engine manufactured by C D Holmes & Co. Her service speed was 11½ knots and she was always an oil-fired tug. Her move to Swansea in 1966 gave her a further three years' service, but in 1969 she was sold and towed to Cork for demolition by Haulbowline Industries Ltd at Passage West.

(Andrew Wiltshire collection)

When the Henry Scarr name was dropped in 1961 the Hessle yard continued to trade under the new title of Richard Dunston (Hessle) Ltd. Between 1961 and 1969 the Ministry of Defence took delivery of 19 twin-screw harbour tugs for use as duty tugs in the Royal Naval dockyards. They were known as the "Dog class" and were named after well-known breeds. The first pair were built by Richard Dunston in 1961 and were named *Airedale* and *Alsatian*. The *Alsatian* was delivered in the October to the Ministry of Defence (Port Auxiliary Service) at Devonport. She had an overall length of 94 feet and her main engines were a pair of Lister Blackstone diesels delivering 1320bhp. She featured twin rudders and had a bollard pull of 16 tonnes. In this view taken at Rosyth on 24 November 1989, the *Alsatian* carries her pennant number A106. She was one of the first examples to be sold and in 1993 passed to Maritime Craft Services, Glasgow. By 1995 she was renamed *Clutha* for Carmet Tugs Ltd and chartered to Klyne Tugs (Lowestoft) Ltd, Lowestoft, who later purchased the tug in 1996. The following year she was briefly with Serco Denholm as *Cumbrae*. After seven years in the ownership of Osprey Maritime Ltd, she left UK waters for West Africa in 2010, having been sold to Akoto Ventures Nigeria Ltd, Lagos.

(Jeff Screeton)

The *Ionia* was another motor tug completed by Henry Scarr Ltd for service on the Thames and had a gross tonnage of 187. She was delivered in August 1960 to William Watkins Ltd, London, and in 1969 she passed to London Tugs Ltd. In 1973 she had a gearbox installed which ensured that ahead and astern movements using her 900bhp British Polar engine could be carried out more quickly. The *Ionia* continued in the Thames with Alexandra Towing Co Ltd from 1975 until 1987, latterly based at Gravesend. In 1987 she was sold to Falmouth Towage Co Ltd and worked at this Cornish port as *St Mawes* until 2001 when she was sold to Captain Andy Anderson. She returned to the River Thames area for intended further service which did not materialise and she was laid up. By 2005 she had moved to a berth at Bideford and carried the name *Ionia* once again. Her condition continued to deteriorate and in 2009 she was sold to Rachael Swain, Bideford, for conversion into a floating café to be called 'Tea on the Tug'. As far as is known this never took place and *Ionia* remains at Bideford awaiting her fate.

(Bernard McCall)

For service at Middlesbrough the **Marton Cross** was a slightly enlarged version of the **Danby Cross** of 1961 which came from the yard of J Pollock & Sons at Faversham. The **Marton Cross** was completed on 25 April 1963 by Richard Dunston. She had a gross tonnage of 133 and an overall length of 93 feet, and was delivered to Wm Crosthwaite & Son for operation by Tees Towing Co Ltd. She was powered by a pair of 6-cylinder Crossley diesels of 1125bhp which were geared through a two-speed reduction gearbox to a single screw rotating, in a steerable Kort nozzle. In 1981 she passed to Sleepdienst Willem Muller at Terneuzen and became **Waasland** in 1982. She was rebuilt with the wheelhouse from another former Tees Towing tug, the **Kamperland** (formerly **Hutton Cross**), which had just been scrapped. This view of the **Waasland** was taken at Ghent on 18 August 1989. It is believed she kept her Crossley engines to the end of her working life, and was thought to have been broken up in about 2009, after latterly working for G J Treffers BV, Haarlem.

(the late John Wiltshire)

The impressive-looking **Indomitable** and **Formidable** were delivered to Alexandra Towing Co Ltd in 1979 primarily for coastal and overseas towing duties. Both were completed by Richard Dunston (Hessle) Ltd and were twin-screw vessels with a gross tonnage of 406. They had an excellent bollard pull of 55 tonnes and their main engines were a pair of 8-cylinder vee-type Ruston-Paxman diesels of 3500bhp. Controllable pitch propellers rotated in Kort nozzles and bow thrusters were fitted. The **Indomitable** had only been in service a matter of weeks when captured at Milford Haven on 20 April 1979. The return to a raised foc's'le is reminiscent of the **Mumbles** of 1969, and a novel feature is the extension of the wheelhouse around the funnel on the port side to provide a clear view of the towing area aft. Initially stationed at Liverpool, the **Indomitable** spent nearly 20 years on charter to the Ministry of Defence stationed in the Falkland Islands during which time her ownership changed from Alexandra Towing to Howard Smith Towage and later Adsteam. In 2006 the **Indomitable** became part of the Svitzer Africa (Pty) Ltd fleet, before returning to the United Kingdom in 2009 as **Hibernia** and working for GPS Marine Contractors Ltd of Chatham.

(Nigel Jones)

Alexandra Towing Company ordered a further six motor tugs in 1964. Three were built by Richard Dunston and were destined for the Southampton fleet while the other trio for the Mersey fleet came from the Northwich yard of W J Yarwood & Sons (see page 46). For 1966 the Mersey fleet received another two new tugs from Dunston, the **Nelson** and **Trafalgar**, which featured the more powerful Crossley HGN8 diesel engine of 1370bhp, giving them each a bollard pull of 21 tonnes. The **Nelson** and **Trafalgar** remained on the Mersey for their entire lives with Alexandra Towing, the **Trafalgar** being reported as sold for further service in 1990. However it was not until 1992 that she had her name shortened to **Fal** for her delivery voyage to Greece. Here she entered service with Megalohari Hellenic Tugboats as **Megalochari VII.** By 1999 she was in service with Vernicos Maritime Co SA as **Agia Marina**, and at this point she had gained a new mast and lost her funnel, which had been replaced with a twin exhaust uptake arrangement incorporating a pair of derricks. This is how we see her on 27 September 2004 off Salamis. She had passed to Turkish shipbreakers at Aliaga by 2011.

(Nigel Jones)

The **Seasider** was the last tug in a series of four conventional single-screw motor tugs built by Richard Dunston for service with Lawson-Batey Tugs Ltd. The final pair comprised the **Holmsider** in June 1984 followed by the **Seasider** in March 1985. In April 1983 Clyde Shipping Company bought out Lawson-Batey Tugs Ltd and the registered owner of the **Seasider** from new was given as Clyde Shipping Co Ltd with Lawson-Batey as her manager. All four were somewhat outdated and underpowered for their age, but obviously deemed suitable for their intended use on the River Tyne and River Wear. The **Seasider** featured a controllable pitch propeller in a steerable Kort nozzle which gave her a bollard pull of 18 tonnes. From 1995 ownership passed to Cory Towage Ltd, and this is the livery in which she is seen at work on the Tyne. In 1999 the **Seasider** was sold to Karapiperis Tug & Salvage of Piraeus and renamed **Karapiperis 16**. By this date her sisters **Wearsider** and **Holmsider** were already at work in Greek waters, but the **Tynesider** had unfortunately foundered in 1994 while working in Loch Fyne.

(Kevin Blair)

Having tried a pair of single-unit Voith-Schneider tractor tugs in 1958 Tees Towing Co Ltd of Middlesbrough settled on single-screw tugs with a steerable Kort rudder for all subsequent deliveries up to 1974. The desire for a more manoeuvrable but compact tug for use on the Tees led to the purchase in 1976 of the **Greatham Cross** and **Skelton Cross**, completed by Scott & Sons of Bowling. These were a pair of distinctive-looking tugs with two forward-mounted azimuthing propellers manufactured by Schottel-Werf of West Germany. The hulls were short at 83 feet but had a breadth of 29 feet and the towing hook was mounted well aft. The **Yarm Cross** was a similar but more powerful tug in 1979, but this time from the Dunston yard while the **Coatham Cross** was a subsequent delivery from Hessle in September 1981. The

Coatham Cross took her power from a pair of Ruston 6RKCM diesels developing 2640bhp and providing a very useful bollard pull of 35 tonnes. The business of Tees Towing Co Ltd passed to Cory Towage Ltd in 1990 who were in turn taken over by Wijsmuller Marine Ltd in 2000 and Svitzer Marine Ltd in 2001. The **Coatham Cross** passed to Fowey Harbour Commissioners as **Cormilan** in 2011, but on 29 April 2014 hit rocks while leaving Fowey and was damaged. She was then sold overseas, and fully repaired she turned up in the Caribbean with Carriacou Yacht Services Ltd in Grenada. She is noted on 18 April 2015 at Phillipsburg, St. Maarten, carrying the new name **La Dani**.

(Danny Lynch)

Established in 1952, Burness Corlett are naval architects who developed amongst other things the principle of the hydroconic hull and we now look at some examples of this patented design which was licensed to a number of British shipyards and used in a number of well-known tugs. The design incorporated a double-chine as opposed to smooth curves, and was intended to improve the passage of water around the hull. The result saw economies in operation as well as a reduction in steel fabricating costs. A small tug with a this type of hull was the **Kingston Buci**, delivered in June 1960 to the Shoreham Harbour Trustees to replace the steam tug **Harold Brown** at the West Sussex port of Shoreham. She was completed by P K Harris & Sons,

Appledore, as a single-screw tug powered by a 6-cylinder Lister Blackstone diesel of 495bhp. At Shoreham she was used to assist the steam bucket dredger **Adur** of 1954, as well as perform general towing duties. She was replaced at Shoreham in 1984 by a new tug, and passed to Poole Harbour Commissioners, where her name was modified to **Kingston Lacy**, a local country house. In 1998 she was sold locally to Jenkins Marine Ltd, and is seen with a tow on 3 September 2000, in lively seas off South Gare in the Tees estuary. In 2016 she is preserved by an enthusiast in the Liverpool area.

(Harry Cutter)

The main shipyard for the construction of tugs incorporating the hydroconic hull was P K Harris & Sons Ltd at Appledore. Virtually all such tugs from this yard were of twin-screw layout and between 145 and 165 tons gross. The subject of this image was originally Dover Harbour Board's **Diligent**. In 1957/58 the Dover Harbour Board replaced its last steam tugs with the twin-screw motor tugs **Diligent** and **Dominant**. Powered by 8-cylinder Lister-Blackstone diesels, they had a bollard pull of 16 tonnes. The pair put in over a quarter of a century of service at Dover and were sold in 1984 to Frank Pearce (Tugs) Ltd, of Poole, at which point they parted company for ever. The **Diligent** was sold to S & H Towage, Gravesend, later being fitted out to undertake fire-fighting. In 1989 she commenced a new life in Canadian waters with Les Remorquages Sorel Inc at Sorel. Here she was renamed **Omni St-Laurent** and this is how we see her on 17 May 1997 at Contrecoeur on the south shore of the St Lawrence River. The fire-fighting monitor is on top of the wheelhouse and she no longer has a lifeboat. Her owner was taken over by Ocean Groupe, Quebec, in 1997 and the tug was sold for breaking up at Ile-aux-Coudres in 2009.

(Marc Piché)

The **Helen M McAllister** was another tug from the Harris yard and was launched in early 1959 as **Stranton** for the British Transport Commission. She was however resold to Canadian owners before completion and towed across to Canada having been purchased by McAllister Towing of Montreal. This was a joint venture between McAllister Brothers of New York and Sogemines of Belgium to provide a towing service on the newly-opened St Lawrence Seaway. She was completed at nearby Sorel and renamed **Helen M McAllister**. A twin-screw tug of 152grt, she was powered by two Lister Blackstone diesels of 1080bhp and had a service speed of 12 knots. She is photographed here at Montreal on 28 January 1975. McAllister Towing of Montreal was acquired by the Ocean Groupe of Quebec in 1997 and the **Helen M McAllister** was renamed **Ocean Golf** in 2000. She eventually underwent a major rebuild transforming her appearance dramatically, as she gained new superstructure including a modern wheelhouse with good all-around visibility. She also received a new pair of General Motors diesels in 2012, which gave her a revised and impressive bollard pull of 34 tonnes.

(René Beauchamp)

The subject of this image, the Greek-owned *Starlet*, was built for Shell-BP Petroleum Development Co of Nigeria Ltd, London, as *Ekole Creek* for Gulf of Guinea service in West Africa. Jointly financed by British Petroleum and the Shell Group, the first oil field in Nigeria was established on a commercial basis in 1956, thus creating a maritime-based export market for crude oil. The *Ekole Creek* was completed in 1959 to support this venture, along with the smaller tug *Elele Creek* and river-based pusher tug *Nzam Creek*. The *Ekole Creek* was fitted with a pair of 8-cylinder Crossley Bros diesels of 960bhp, and as can

be seen, was equipped for fire-fighting. In 1971 she was purchased by Piraeus-based tug owner Loucas G Matsas, and in 1974 was re-engined with a pair of Klöckner-Humboldt-Deutz diesels that were new in 1962. She is seen here in Greek waters at Patras in 1990, the title of her owner having become Loucas G Matsas Salvage & Towage Maritime Co from 1986. The *Starlet* was still giving good service and is instantly recognisable in 2015 when her owner was recorded as Maril Naftiki Eteria and still registered in Piraeus.

(Alan Sparrow)

A second hull bearing the name **Stranton** was launched in 1959 at Appledore , and this was completed in November 1959 for the state-owned British Transport Commission to be based at West Hartlepool. She was the third of a class of four identical twin-screw tugs built by P K Harris for service at this port, the others being the **Hart**, **Seaton** and finally **Throston**. The **Throston** was sold overseas in 1961, and the remaining three came under the control of the British Transport Docks Board which had been established by the Transport Act of 1962. In 1966 control of the docks at West Hartlepool passed to the Tees and Hartlepool Port Authority, and the **Seaton** was sold to Italian owners in 1972, reflecting a downturn in traffic at the port. The **Stranton** along with the **Hart** continued to serve Hartlepool until 1995 when they were both sold to Bilberry Shipping & Stevedores at Waterford. It was intended to give the **Stranton** a new name, **Hook Head**, but it is thought this never took place. She was soon sold on, eventually passing to Lebanese owners in 1998 as **Stranton**. She was noted at work in Greek waters in 2015 as **Panagia Soumela** and in superb condition for her 56 years. This view of her at Hartlepool dates from 27 October 1989.

(Harry Cutter)

A similar tug from P K Harris was delivered to the British Transport Commission in May 1960 for use at the port of Newhaven in Sussex. Named **Meeching** after an area in Newhaven, she replaced the steam tug **Foremost 22** which dated from 1924. The **Meeching** was a 12 knot, twin-screw vessel with an overall length of 96 feet and powered by two 8-cylinder Lister Blackstone Marine diesels. She was normally used to handle ferries and general cargo ships at the port, but occasionally ventured beyond Newhaven. The **Meeching** had a fire-fighting and salvage capability and could be used to respond to vessels in distress. Her owners became the British Railways Board, and she was managed by Sealink UK Ltd from 1979. She is seen entering the River Ouse at Newhaven in 1982. In 1989 the **Meeching** passed with the port to the Sea Containers Group and still continued to function as the primary port tug, latterly operated by Subsearch Marine. After nearly 40 years at Newhaven she was sold in 2000 to Tug Manning Ltd, Gravesend, for coastal towing but eventually fell out of use. In 2012 she passed to N E Murray, of Queenborough, for renovation and took the new name **Nore Crest**. She was still hard at work in 2016.

(the late John Wiltshire collection)

A small number of hydroconic hull tugs were completed as single-screw vessels and Belfast-based tug operator John Cooper (Belfast) Ltd had several examples. The first was the **Carrickfergus** of 1958, completed by P K Harris, while in 1959 there followed a much larger pair of 207grt from the Gateshead shipyard of T Mitchison. Named **Cashel** and **Clonmel**, they were fitted for fire-fighting and were based at Cobh for use at the Whitegate Oil Refinery. This new facility opened in 1959 and was a joint venture between Shell, Texaco, BP and Esso. In 1969 John Cooper was taken over by R & J H Rea Ltd, and in 1970 the Rea fleet passed to Cory Ship Towage Ltd. In 1973 the **Clonmel**

transferred to Cory Ship Towage (Clyde) Ltd, Glasgow, becoming **Cruiser**, and eventually moved to the Newport fleet in South Wales. The **Cruiser** is seen in the lock at Newport on 7 April 1980. The tug alongside is the **Wyegarth**, another tug with a hydroconic hull, and which was new to the British Transport Commission at Newport as **St Woolos** in 1960. Both tugs were sold later in 1980, the **Cruiser** eventually finding a new home in Cornwall with Falmouth Towage Co Ltd as **St Gluvias**. Sold in 2003 she was later reported to be awaiting conversion to a houseboat at Hoo Marina in Kent.

(the late John Wiltshire)

Oil terminals, container terminals and deep water bulk cargo terminals can be found around the coast of the UK and these facilities required powerful and often purpose-built tugs. Our attention now turns to such tugs. Milford Haven in Pembrokeshire is a large sheltered natural waterway, and deemed an ideal site for oil terminals and refineries. The first of these opened in 1960, and to coincide with this, the towage contract was awarded to R & J H Rea Ltd. They ordered four large tugs from Henry Scarr at Hessle two of which, **Stackgarth** and **Thorngarth** of 1959, were equipped for fire-fighting. The **Anglegarth** and **Dalegarth** arrived in 1960 and at 306 tons gross were impressive modern-looking tugs of 1300bhp. In 1964/65 they were joined by a trio of similar tugs,

but this time from Richards Shipbuilders at Lowestoft. The **Anglegarth** is noted on the buoys in Milford Haven on 23 May 1970, shortly before all seven passed to Cory Ship Towage Ltd. A further trio of new tugs in 1970 rendered some of the original quartet surplus, and they were transferred overseas to other contract work. The **Anglegarth** was chartered to Smit International (Antilles) in 1972 for use at Willemstad, returning to the UK in 1976, whereupon she eventually took up residence at Avonmouth. She was sold in 1979 to Greek owners Andreas & George Kyrtatas, becoming **Leon**. She was still in service in early 2016 with another owner in the Piraeus area.

(the late John Wiltshire)

Located on the Firth of Forth, the Hound Point terminal was opened in 1975. It is owned by BP and is a loading point for North Sea crude oil that arrives at the nearby Dalmeny storage facility via the Fortes pipeline. Four large tugs were built to service this. Robb Caledon at Leith completed the **Boquhan** and **Duchray** in 1975 and these were equipped for fire-fighting. They were followed in 1976 by the **Almond** and **Kelty** from Richards Shipbuilders. The **Boquhan** shows off her distinctive exhaust uptakes and fire-fighting platforms in this view from 21 July 1983. All four tugs were initially operated by Grangemouth & Forth Towing Co Ltd, which from 1977 changed its identity to Forth Tugs Ltd. The **Boquhan** had a grt of 326 and was powered by a 12-cylinder vee-type Ruston Paxman diesel of 2680bhp driving a controllable pitch propeller. By 1997 the contract at Hound Point passed to Targe Towing Ltd who purchased new and much more powerful tugs and the original four were sold off. In 1997 the **Boquhan** passed to Divemex Ltd and was renamed **Oliver** for service in West African waters. Having changed her name to **Nano**, she was sailing under the Panamanian flag from 2009, but was reported out of use at Lagos two years later.

(the late Des Harris)

Cory Ship Towage were successful in obtaining a towage contract for Gulf's Point Tupper refinery in Nova Scotia, Canada, in 1970 requiring three tugs. A partnership with L Smit's International of Rotterdam led to the creation of Smit-Cory International Port Towage which then gained a contract to serve the Come-By-Chance refinery in Newfoundland. Two new tugs were delivered to Point Tupper in 1971 as the **Point Tupper** and **Point Melford**. The Come-By-Chance refinery then benefitted from four new tugs; the **Point James** and **Point Gilbert** in 1972, followed by the larger **Point Carroll** and **Point Spencer** in 1973. All were completed in the UK and the **Point Carroll** was built at the Richard Dunston yard. She had a gross tonnage of 366 and was powered by a 12-cylinder vee Ruston Paxman diesel engine of 3300bhp. Both refineries closed down between 1976 and 1980 and the six tugs were re-allocated to work elsewhere. The **Point Carroll** remained in Canadian waters and was operating in the eastern Canada fleet at Halifax until 2001. At this stage she was sold to McKeil Work Boats, Toronto, as **Tony Mackay** and is thought to be still in service. In this view she is noted near Montreal on 19 August 1976 in the colours of Smit-Cory International.

(René Beauchamp)

Felixstowe's first container terminal opened in 1967 and by the early 1990s it had become one of Europe's major container ports. In March 1990 Alexandra Towing Co Ltd took delivery of a powerful azimuthing stern drive tug from the Great Yarmouth yard of Richards Shipbuilders. Intended specifically for use at Felixstowe, she was named **Deben** and was fitted for fire-fighting. She featured a pair of Aquamaster propulsion units and these gave her a bollard pull of 43 tonnes. Twelve months later an identical tug was delivered to Felixstowe from the same yard, and entered service as **Trimley**. As mentioned earlier, Alexandra Towing passed to Howard Smith Towage Ltd in 1993 and then to Adsteam (UK) Ltd in 2001. The **Trimley** remained stationed at Felixstowe becoming **Adsteam Trimley** in 2006. Later that year she passed with the Adsteam business to Svitzer Towage Ltd, and was renamed **Svitzer Trimley** in 2007. Leaving Felixstowe she was based at Lowestoft for a number of years with associated fleet Felixarc, before moving to Lisbon in 2013/2014 as **Svitzer Trave**. She returned to UK waters again in 2014 and back under UK registry she became **Svitzer Trimley** once more, based at Immingham. She is recorded at work on the lower Humber on 27 September 2015.

(Simon Smith)

From 1986 Cory Panama Corp commenced a contract to supply tugs for service at the Puerto Armuelles terminal in Panama which it had managed since 1985. Initially they chartered five tugs to work this terminal, but later sent the **Brigadier** out from the UK and placed an order for two newbuilds. These would be fire-fighting, anchor-handling tugs and both were constructed by Cochrane Shipbuilders Ltd of Selby. The **Maria Isabel I** was the first completed in July 1987 followed a few months later by the **Maria Luisa II**. These were vessels of 376grt and fitted with a pair of azimuthing propellers producing a bollard pull of 60 tonnes. They were delivered to Cory Towage (Panama) Ltd and placed under Panamanian registry. By 1996 the contract at Puerto Armuelles had terminated and the two tugs eventually went on charter to Smit International in Panama. The **Maria Isabel I** was sold in 1998 while her sister returned to the UK, passing to Wijsmuller Marine Ltd in 2000. The **Maria Luisa II** is seen out on the Milford Haven waterway in full Wijsmuller colours, having been just drydocked at nearby Milford dock. She passed into Svitzer Marine ownership in 2002. In 2016 she was working for owners in Argentina.

(Danny Lynch)

The **Ganges** was the very last conventional single-screw motor tug constructed for the Alexandra Towing Co Ltd and was also its first tug completed specifically for service at Felixstowe. She was delivered from the Dunston shipyard in May 1982 and was registered in Harwich. She had a gross tonnage of 281 and was powered by a 12-cylinder Ruston 12RK270 diesel developing 2640bhp, driving a controllable pitch propeller in a directional nozzle. As can be seen from this spectacular view of her on 29 April 1984, she was equipped with a fire-fighting capability. Upon absorption into the Howard Smith Towage group in 1993 she was soon transferred to the Gravesend fleet, ultimately passing to Adsteam UK. When sold in 2005 she had been one of the last conventional tugs left operating in the Adsteam fleet, and found a new owner in Northern Ireland with Foyle Marine Services. They renamed her **Culmore** and fitted her with a retractable directional bow-thruster. She is still in service at Londonderry in 2016.

(the late John Wiltshire)

Esso have operated an oil refinery at Fawley on the Solent since 1925, and in 2016 it is still a major site for the import of crude oil and distribution of products such as petroleum, LPG, aviation fuel and lubricating oil, with about 25% leaving by ship. Southampton-based Red Funnel served the oil terminal at Fawley for many years and in 1970 took delivery of two purpose-built fire-fighting tugs, *Gatcombe* and *Vecta*, to replace older and smaller tugs. Completed by Richard Dunston, they were, unusually for Red Funnel, single-screw tugs, and featured a Simon Snorkel hydraulic fire-fighting platform mounted on top of the wheelhouse. The *Gatcombe* was delivered in November 1970 to the Southampton, Isle of Wight & South of England Royal Mail Steam Packet Co at Southampton, and had an impressive bollard pull of 45 tonnes. The *Gatcombe* is seen here in her earlier colours at the oil terminal. In 1994 the contract for towage and fire-fighting support at Fawley passed to Solent Towage, a subsidiary of Østensjø Rederi AS. The *Gatcombe* and *Vecta* were eventually sold in 1997 and 1999 respectively. They passed to Multratug BV at Terneuzen becoming *Multratug 6* and *Multratug 8* respectively. In 2016 both tugs are still at work.

(the late John Wiltshire collection)

A new deep water tidal harbour was built at Port Talbot in South Wales to accommodate large bulk carriers with cargoes of iron ore and coal for the nearby steelworks. It opened in 1970 and in time for this event Alexandra Towing Co Ltd had taken delivery of *Mumbles*, a large purpose-built tug. She was delivered in February 1969 from Richard Dunston at Hessle with a gross tonnage of 291 and was powered by a 9-cylinder Ruston 9ATCM engine of 2190bhp. She was registered in Swansea, and in addition to her normal port towage duties at Swansea and Port Talbot, her substantial raised fo'c'sle and her power made her an ideal tug to perform coastal towing. The *Mumbles* was joined at Swansea in 1970 by a second new tug, *Margam*, which was also intended for work at the tidal harbour. When Howard Smith Towage Ltd took over Alexandra Towing in 1993, the *Mumbles* continued to work at Swansea until 1998 when she was sold to T P Towage Ltd, Gibraltar, where she worked as a harbour tug until 2009. Since then she has been sailing under the Portuguese flag as *Guardiao* for Lutamar of Setubal. In this view the *Mumbles* is seen off Swansea on the hazy morning of 15 April 1991.

(Andrew Wiltshire)

To replace older tugs four more powerful vessels were ordered in 1974 by Cory Ship Towage Ltd for the Milford Haven fleet. Two were completed by Richards Shipbuilders at Great Yarmouth while the second pair were ordered from one of the Drypool Shipbuilding Group yards, and were fitted for fire-fighting. The first pair entered service in 1976 as **Edengarth** and **Eskgarth** and were joined at the same time by **Exegarth** from the yard of Beverley Shipbuilding and Engineering. This yard then closed down and the contract for the fourth tug was taken on by Richards who eventually completed her as **Eyegarth** in 1977. All four were registered as owned by Rea Towing Co of Liverpool. They had a bollard pull of 50 tonnes, but were conventional screw tugs with a controllable pitch propeller. Ownership of the **Edengarth** passed to Irish Tugs Ltd (Cory Ship Towage Ltd) in 1983 and ten years later she was equipped for fire-fighting, for use at Cork along with **Eskgarth**. In between **Edengarth** had a spell in the Mersey fleet wearing the funnel colours of Rea Towing. Here we see her off Liverpool on 12 May 1988, after aborting the docking of the bulk carrier **Sounion**. The **Edengarth** transferred to Avonmouth briefly in 1997 and was sold in 1999. After a number of subsequent owners it is believed that she was sailing in 2015 as **Prawira Dua** under the Indonesian flag.

(Paul Boot)

The **Lyndhurst** was a large tractor tug built for service at Southampton where her size and power were required for ship handling at the port's container terminal. Container ships continued to increase in size during the 1990s, and unlike the container port at Felixstowe, Southampton is subject to greater tidal fluctuations and the passage to the berths requires careful manoeuvring. The **Lyndhurst** was completed at the yard of McTay Marine Ltd, Bromborough, having been launched in January 1996. She was delivered in the April to Howard Smith Towage Ltd at Southampton and had a gross tonnage of 379. She was based on the same design as the six tugs that entered service with

Howard Smith on the Humber between 1990 and 1996. The **Lyndhurst** was fitted for fire-fighting and designed to operate with an un-manned engine room. Her main engines were a pair of 6-cylinder Ruston-Paxman 6RK270M diesels developing 4016bhp and which drove a pair of Voith-Schneider propulsion units.The **Lyndhurst** is seen in the Solent in September 1997. In 2001 ownership passed to Adsteam Towage Ltd and she was renamed **Adsteam Lyndhurst** in 2006. A second change of name to **Svitzer Lyndhurst** took place in 2007, and in 2016 she was based at Grangemouth.

(Bernard McCall)

Our next set of images looks at tugs built at inland shipyards. William Cory and Son Ltd operated a number of tug fleets on the Rivers Thames and Medway and these included Mercantile Lighterage Ltd and Cory Tank Lighterage Ltd. In 1952 the latter took delivery of a pair of lighterage tugs, **Recruit** and **Swiftstone**, which were employed towing tank barges to wharves on the Thames, and were of a low profile to enable them to pass under the numerous bridges upstream from Tower Bridge. The pair were built by Richard Dunston whose yard at Thorne was located on the north bank of the Stainforth and Keadby Canal, and some 45 miles from the sea. It was however ideal for the construction of small vessels and many tugs were built at this yard over the years. This view of **Recruit** heading down the Thames and passing St Johns Wharf was taken on 12 April 1980. She had an overall length of 80 feet and was powered by a 670bhp Crossley diesel. In 1983 the **Recruit** was transferred to another subsidiary company, Cory Waste Management Ltd, which in 1990 became Cory Environmental Ltd, London. Still going strong, the **Recruit** was refurbished in 1996 when she was re-engined and a new wheelhouse and twin funnels were fitted. She was sold in 2011 and by 2013 had passed into the fleet of GPS Marine, and was given the traditional Thames tug name **GPS Cervia**, for continued service on the Thames.

(the late John Wiltshire)

William James Yarwood commenced building ships towards the end of the 19th century at Northwich, on the Weaver Navigation. Succeeded by his sons, this yard continued to build numerous small vessels including tugs and coasters. Between the years 1955 and 1965, it built 32 tugs for service at home and abroad. When R & J H Rea Ltd decided to modernise its Avonmouth-based fleet, an order was placed with the Yarwood yard for a pair of motor tugs. The first to be completed was *Plumgarth* in February 1960 followed in June by *Avongarth*. These were single-screw tugs powered by an 8-cylinder Ruston & Hornsby diesel of 960bhp, and they had an overall length of 96 feet. An interesting feature was the addition of an open flying bridge, and this was regularly used in fine weather, offering the skipper greater all-round visibility during towing operations. The *Plumgarth* transferred to Cardiff in 1963 and passed to Cory Ship Towage Ltd in 1970. From mid-1979 she was paired up with the *Avongarth* once again when they were both based at Plymouth. *Plumgarth* was sold in 1985 eventually passing to Greek owners at Heraklion, Crete. She can still be found at work there as the *Minotavros* in 2016, and is maintained in superb order. In her Cory Towage days *Plumgarth* is seen off Barry on 28 July 1970.

(the late John Wiltshire)

Founded at Hull in 1883, Cook, Welton and Gemmell was occupying a yard at Grovehill, Beverley, by 1902. The bulk of their work was trawlers but a number of tugs were built over the years. In 1955 Overseas Towage and Salvage Co Ltd, of London, took delivery of the compact ocean-going tug *Marinia* from the yard. She was of 392grt and with an overall length of 129 feet was the third Overseas Towage and Salvage tug to carry this name. She had two British Polar engines geared to a single screw and her overall power output was a mere 960bhp. She gave her owners just eleven years' service and was sold to Selco (Singapore) Ltd, Singapore, in 1966 where she became *Salvana*. This is how we see her on 26 February 1976. She passed to Philippine owners Transpac Marine SA in 1981, and continued to work, but under the Panamanian flag as *Maranaw*. She was finally broken up at Manila in 1987. Meanwhile Cook, Welton and Gemmell was taken over by C D Holmes in 1963, which then became part of the Drypool Group in 1973.

(Andrew Wiltshire collection)

The purchase of the steam tugs *Canada*, *Formby* and *Gladstone* in 1951 saw the start of the post-war fleet modernisation programme for the Alexandra Towing Co Ltd. At around 237grt they were quite large tugs that were loosely based along the lines of certain Empire tugs constructed during WWII. The *Canada* and *Formby* were completed by Cochrane & Sons Ltd, Selby, and delivered in July 1951 with the *Gladstone* following in September. All three were coal-fired and had 1000ihp triple expansion machinery giving them a speed of 12 knots. Initially based at Liverpool, *Gladstone* moved to Southampton in 1952 followed in 1956 by *Canada*. The *Gladstone* had her boiler converted to oil-firing in 1956, while the other pair were dealt with in 1960. Subsequently all three lost one of their lifeboats and had their funnels and masts reduced in height which gave them a more balanced appearance. The *Formby* remained on the Mersey until about 1967, when she moved to Swansea. This is where we see her in the Kings Dock approaching the lock in glorious afternoon sunshine. In 1969 the *Formby* and *Canada* were sold to Fratelli Barretta fu Domenico, Brindisi, and renamed *Poderoso* and *Strepitoso* respectively. The *Strepitoso* was eventually broken up in late 1988, and it is believed that the *Poderoso* underwent a similar fate at around this time.

(the late Des Harris)

Isaac Pimblott & Sons was another shipbuilder who was based at Northwich. The business was founded in 1867 and eventually settled down at a yard near Hunts Lock by 1906. Like W J Yarwood, they built small craft and a number of tugs, including four Improved Girl class examples for the Ministry of Defence (R.M.A.S.) in 1966/67. The yard finally closed in 1971. The Improved Girl class consisted of nine tugs, the Pimblott contribution being *Celia*, *Charlotte*, *Christine* and *Clare*. The remainder were completed by Richard Dunston at their Thorne shipyard. They would be dockyard based and upon completion,

the *Celia* and *Clare* were despatched to the naval bases at Singapore and Hong Kong respectively. The *Christine* was based at Devonport and was powered by a 6-cylinder Lister-Blackstone engine of 495bhp. She was sold out of naval service in 1990 passing to Seastructures Ltd, Plymouth, and was engaged on engineering contracts. As such she is noted sailing from Barry on a windy 6 July 1993. The *Christine* was operating for Alan Pratt of Rainham, Kent, by 2006 and was last noted as such in 2016.

(Nigel Jones)

Charles D Holmes & Co Ltd was a marine engineering company based in Hull and a well known manufacturer of steam plant and boilers for small ships such as tugs and trawlers. During the 1960s they built a number of tugs at a yard in Beverley, which they had taken over from Cook, Welton and Gemmell in 1963. These included four similar twin-screw tugs of 2400bhp for United Towing Co Ltd at Hull. They took the names **Seaman**, **Superman** and **Yorkshireman** which arrived in 1967, and concluded with **Hullman** in May 1968. The latter had a tragically short career being sunk off Immingham in 1969. She was soon raised and put back into service, but was lost in 1971 after being struck by her tow in the North Sea. Our image is of the **Seaman**, which is seen making her way along the New Waterway in July 1976. The **Seaman** was sold to Venezuelan owners in 1978 followed by **Superman** in 1979, the pair becoming **Vesca R-5** and **Vesca R-6** respectively for Venecia Ship Service C.A., Puerto Cabello. Both were believed to have become derelict by 2010.

(the late Les Ring)

With its yard located 60 miles from the sea at Gainsborough on the River Trent, J S Watson (Gainsborough) Ltd was noted for constructing tugs, fishing boats, pontoons and barges. They built six Birch class Empire-type steam tugs between 1942 and 1946. The **Empire Mustang** was completed in August 1943 for the Ministry of War Transport and registered at Hull. She was 113 feet long, of 242 grt, and powered by a 1000ihp triple expansion steam engine. In 1947 she passed to Tees Towing Co Ltd of Middlesbrough who renamed her **Dundas Cross**. After eleven years she was sold to Newport Screw Towing Co Ltd, where she became **Duneagle**. Here she was the first of three former Empire-type tugs operated, but was the odd one out having a coal-fired boiler. This may explain why she was the first to be sold in 1965. The **Duneagle** passed to Greek owner Tsavliris (Salvage & Towage) Co Ltd, Piraeus, and was renamed **Nisos Syros**. This view of her was taken in May 1973, by which time she had gained a wheelhouse on her previously open flying bridge. In 1975 she was sold to Maritime & Commercial Enterprises Ltd, also of Piraeus, and was broken up the following year.

(the late John Wiltshire collection)

This image was taken in striking winter sunshine at Swansea on 4 December 1973. The photographer was most fortunate in capturing the Liverpool-based tug *Egerton* at work during her very short spell at Swansea. When the Alexandra Towing Company ordered six motor tugs in 1964, three of them were completed by W J Yarwood & Sons at Northwich. The **Langton** entered service in November 1964 followed by **Egerton** and **Brocklebank** in April and December 1965 respectively. The **Egerton** had a speed of 12 knots and was powered by a Crossley diesel of 1200bhp, but unlike some earlier Alexandra tugs of this size, she had a fixed-pitch propeller. She transferred to Felixstowe in 1976 and was joined by **Langton** in 1978. The latter was sold in 1986 but the **Egerton** continued to work at the Suffolk port until 1990, when she was replaced by the new ASD tug **Deben**. The **Egerton** was then sold to Oil Transport Company of Santo Domingo in the Dominican Republic and was renamed **Caribe I**. She is thought to be no longer in existence.

(the late John Wiltshire)

There was a time when the east coast of the UK could boast a large number of shipyards both large and small. Most were located on rivers and estuaries and many lay close to a port. Our attention now turns to some of these yards. Lowestoft was home to Richards (Shipbuilders) whose history can be traced back to a boatyard established in the town in 1876. R & J H Rea Ltd took delivery of four motor tugs from this yard in 1966 to replace ageing steam tugs at Cardiff and Barry. They were in order of delivery, the **Butegarth**, **Uskgarth**, **Danegarth** and **Bargarth**, and were based on the similar **Lowgarth** of 1965. They were single-screw vessels powered by a Blackstone diesel of 860bhp driving a fixed-pitch propeller in a steerable Kort nozzle. The **Bargarth** is seen at work in the lock at Cardiff in the winter sun of 9 January 1983. She carries the livery of Cory Ship Towage Ltd following the 1970 takeover of R & J H Rea Ltd. In 1986 the **Bargarth** was selected for conversion to an open-combi tug. She had a retractable Aquamaster bow thruster installed that increased her bollard pull from 14 to 17 tonnes. She survived long enough with Cory to pass into Wijsmuller Marine ownership from 2000 and then Svitzer Marine Ltd in 2001. The **Bargarth** was then sold to Bilberry Shipping & Stevedores Ltd, Waterford, in 2002 under Irish registry. In 2009 she became **Tennaherdhya** and was registered in the Scilly Isles for Marine Asset Management Ltd, later moving to Keynvor Morlift Ltd, Appledore.

(Andrew Wiltshire)

A most unusual vessel was constructed in 1966 by James W Cook (Wivenhoe) Ltd of Wivenhoe, Essex, for the Port of London Authority. She was a purpose-built pusher tug of 189grt, and named **Broodbank** after Sir Joseph G Broodbank, the Chairman of the Dock and Warehouse Committee of the Port of London Authority from 1909 to 1920. She was a short vessel at 56 feet but had a substantial beam of 31 feet. She was a particularly manoeuvrable tug being fitted with a pair of Schottel SRP 225 azimuthing propulsion units, powered by a pair of Rolls-Royce DV8TM turbocharged diesel engines of 1000bhp. She is seen on the Thames working with a dredger off the Royal Docks on 22 July 1973. Upon her sale in 1994 to Briggs Marine Contractors Ltd of Burntisland, her appearance changed dramatically. During 1995 the **Broodbank** was rebuilt into a workboat and had a large forward section of hull added. She also received a new superstructure, and her overall length increased to 93 feet. Renamed **Forth Constructor** for her new lease of life, she went on to receive a pair of new Daewoo diesels in 2003, which now powered a pair of Ulstein directional propellers.

(the late C C Beazley)

48

Founded in 1946, Humber - St. Andrew's Engineering Co Ltd are still in business as marine engineers and naval architects. In the 1960s they were based at St. Andrew's Dock in Hull, and built a handful of tugs including a group of four twin-screw vessels for United Towing Co Ltd. Delivery of these commenced in February 1963, with the *Trawlerman*, followed by *Tidesman* in June, *Tugman* in October 1964, and finally *Motorman* in February 1965. They were powered by a pair of 6-cylinder Lister Blackstone Marine diesels with a combined output of 782bhp, and featured twin exhaust uptakes in place of a funnel. From 1970 all four were managed by Humber Tugs Ltd, Hull, who became their owners from 1978. This is a view of the *Tidesman* at work off Hull. She was the first example to be sold passing to Greek owners Alexander G Tsavliris & Sons Maritime Company in 1981 as *Hector*. At a later date she received new engines and is believed to be still in service in 2015 as *Christos XVII*. Her three sisters passed to Klyne Tugs at Lowestoft between 1983 and 1985. The *Motorman* eventually went on to become a luxury yacht, but the continued existence of *Trawlerman* and *Tugman* is in doubt.

(Laurie Schofield)

The history of Brook Marine Ltd, Lowestoft, can be traced back to the 19th century. From 1954 they occupied a new shipyard which built many small vessels for both civilian and naval customers. The civilian ships completed included trawlers, yachts, lifeboats and a couple of tugs for service in New Zealand. The *Raumanga* and her sister *Parahaki* were delivered in July 1963 to Whangarei Harbour Board at Whangarei. They had a substantial fire-fighting capability and were intended for use at the new Marsden Point oil refinery which opened in 1964. At 376grt these were big single-screw tugs and had diesel-electric propulsion. Two 8-cylinder diesel engines drove two 600kw generators supplying power to one 1500shp motor geared to a single-screw. In 1979 the Whangarei Harbour Board changed its title to Northland Harbour Board, and in 1988 both tugs were sold after being replaced by a pair of large Voith-Schneider tractor tugs. The *Raumanga* and *Parahaki* were purchased by Ocean Towage & Salvage (David Brown) at Brisbane and allegedly took the names *Stanley Brown* and *Alfred Brown* respectively. However on 27 March 1990 at Fremantle, the *Raumanga* is showing no sign of her allocated name *Stanley Brown*. It is reported that she still survived as recently as 2006.

(the late John Wiltshire collection)

After being involved with repair work for many years, the Yorkshire Dry Dock Co Ltd, of Hull, began shipbuilding during the 1960s building small coasters and tank barges. One of the last vessels built was the twin-unit Voith-Schneider tug **Redbridge** which was completed in August 1995 for Isle of Wight and South of England, Royal Mail Steam Packet Plc (Red Funnel) of Southampton. She was reputed to have cost in the region of £3.5 million, a loss-making figure for the shipyard. With a bollard pull of 45 tonnes, she was a powerful addition to the fleet. In 2001 her owners were restyled Red Funnel Towage Ltd, and the following year the business passed to Adsteam Towage (Southampton) Ltd. The **Redbridge** was renamed **Adsteam Redbridge** in 2005 and following the takeover by Svitzer Towage Ltd in 2006 she eventually took the name **Svitzer Redbridge** during 2008. She is still in service with Svitzer in 2016, and has latterly been part of the Tyne-based fleet.

(Douglas Cromby)

The **Sotirios** is another former Empire tug and makes an interesting comparison with the **Flying Kestrel** on page 23. She was an example of the Warrior class, and was completed on the River Tyne in August 1942 by Clelands (Successors) Ltd at Wallsend as **Empire Piper** for the Ministry of War Transport. She was powered by a 1000ihp triple expansion steam engine and her boiler was coal-fired. She passed out of naval service in 1946 and was sold to John Cooper to work at Belfast. She was renamed **Piper**. In 1963 **Piper** was sent to the shipyard of T Mitchison at Gateshead to be converted to a motor tug but the conversion did not take place because the Seawork Group, to which the yard belonged, became bankrupt in 1962. In 1969 Cooper was taken over by R & J H Rea Ltd and in 1970 Cory Ship Towage (Northern Ireland) Ltd was established. The **Piper** was the only steam tug absorbed into the new Cory Ship Towage group. She was sold in 1971, ultimately passing to A P Papayanis and registered in Piraeus. In this view she has been seen in May 1973 at Heraklion on Crete. Now named **Sotirios**, it looks like she has just been given a complete repaint. She was laid up out of use by 1982, and was sold for breaking up in 1987 as **Lalrion**.

(the late T W Wiltshire)

Another tug built at Wallsend was **Andy Mitchell** which was completed in 1968 for Wimpey Marine Ltd (George Wimpey) for service at Bahrain, and was registered in London. She came from the yard of Clelands Shipbuilding Co Ltd, and as built had a gross tonnage of 243. Clelands had been owned by Swan Hunter since 1967 and after nationalisation, the yard closed down in 1984. The **Andy Mitchell** was a powerful twin-screw tug with an overall length of 101 feet. Her engines were of Ruston & Hornsby manufacture driving controllable pitch propellers and she had a speed of 13 knots. After just five years she returned to northern Europe and was sold to Willem Muller Nederland B.V. of Terneuzen under the Dutch flag and became **Engeland**. She is seen on the New Waterway on 25 August 1980. She was operating in Greek waters the following year as **Skyros** for Architug Shipping SA, Piraeus, and went on to sail under a number of different flags including those of Honduras and Belize. She was last reported sailing as **MS Trat** in 2012 and owned by BSL Leasing Company of Bangkok.

(the late Les Ring)

Rowhedge is a village in Essex located downstream from Colchester on the River Colne. Rowhedge Ironworks Co Ltd built around 900 small vessels from 1904 until closure, and these included coasters and ferries, but very few tugs. Two of the Ministry of Defence Dog class tugs were constructed at Rowhedge around about the time the yard ceased building ships in 1964. They were **Collie** and **Corgi** and it is believed that both tugs were actually completed by L.S.B. Engineering Co, Lowestoft. They were in most respects standard Dog class twin-screw tugs powered by a pair of 8-cylinder Lister Blackstone diesels of 1320bhp and with a speed of $10\frac{1}{2}$ knots. The **Corgi** was allocated pennant number A330 and was based at Rosyth until her transfer to Devonport in 1978. She continued here and in 1997 both her engines received a major rebuild. The **Corgi** was then sold to Seastructures Ltd, Plymouth, and was engaged on construction contract work around the UK. It is in this role that she is recorded at Cardiff on 22 July 1998. Four years later she passed to a Greek owner and was often to be found working out of Lemnos as **Molossos** for Issalos Shipping Co, Athens.

(the late John Wiltshire)

In September 1923 the single-screw steam tug **Kerse** was delivered to Grangemouth & Forth Towing Co Ltd, a company that had been operating tugs at the port of Grangemouth on the Forth estuary since 1895. She was completed in Leith by John Cran & Sommerville Ltd, who had a reputation for building tugs for service at home and overseas. The business was established in 1917 by marine engineer John Cran & Co, in partnership with R A Sommerville. It was a fairly short-lived business, being sold to Henry Robb of Leith in 1929. This view of the **Kerse** out on the Firth of Forth dates from October 1967. She was a vessel of 214 gross tons with an overall length of 107 feet and powered by an 800ihp compound steam engine. Apart from a brief spell of war service during WWII, she spent her entire working life based at Grangemouth. She was not withdrawn until 1974 whereupon she passed to P & W MacLellan Ltd, Bo'ness, for breaking up. In 1972 the Grangemouth & Forth Towing Co Ltd was purchased 50:50 by Cory Ship Towage and Clyde Shipping Co but retained its identity.

(Alastair Paterson)

J P Rennoldson and Sons had a shipyard at South Shields on the River Tyne from 1850. They built mostly smaller ships and specialised in building tugs. The yard closed down in 1929 due to a downturn in orders. A steam tug was completed in 1909 for service in Australia with William Fenwick, Sydney. The tug was launched as **Advance**, but was completed in April 1909 as **Heroic**, and she was mortgaged to the Commercial Banking Co Ltd, Sydney. She was a single-screw vessel of 268 gross tons and with an overall length of 131 feet and a breadth of 24 feet. Her machinery consisted of a 1000ihp triple-expansion engine constructed by the shipyard. Her boiler was coal-fired and she had a speed of 11 knots. From 1914 her registered owner was J Fenwick & Co Ltd, Sydney. She returned to UK waters during the WWI for Admiralty service, and was in use at Devonport and the Scilly Isles as the rescue tug **Epic** from 1917. She was back in Sydney by 1920 and soon regained her name **Heroic**. As such she continued to operate for J Fenwick & Co Ltd who eventually became her official owner, until being retired in about 1967. The **Heroic** was sold to a local breaker who failed to complete the demolition, and she became a derelict hulk at Rozelle Bay where she remains in 2016.

(World Ship Photo Library)

The Voith-Schneider cycloidal propeller has become an increasingly popular method of propulsion in tugs since the 1950s. We look at some examples of tugs thus powered. It was developed in 1926 by the Austrian engineer Ernst Schneider, who was working for the German engineering firm of J M Voith. They would normally be mounted as either a single unit or a pair, at approximately one third of the length from the tug's bows. A fixed skeg is mounted towards the stern and takes the place of a conventional rudder. A class of twelve small single-unit tractor tugs was built by Richard Dunston Ltd, Thorne, for the Ministry of Defence (Port Auxiliary Service) in 1972/73. Known as the Triton class, they were based on four tugs built between 1963 and 1966 for The Hull Steam Trawlers Mutual Insurance & Protecting Co. All twelve tugs took girls' names and with a crew of four would be used for moving barges and assisting cold moves within dockyards. One example was **Joan** which was based at Portsmouth where she served along with **Irene**, **Isabel**, **Norah** and later **Joyce**. These tugs had an overall length of 60 feet and a beam of 17 feet and were powered by a 4-cylinder Lister Blackstone diesel of 330bhp which gave them a speed of 8 knots. All were eventually sold out of naval service and **Joan** passed to Baker Marine Ltd of Southampton retaining her name **Joan**. In this view she is seen at Portsmouth Naval Dockyard on 21 May 1988 with the **Norah** and **Irene** for company.

(the late John Wiltshire)

Sullom Voe is an oil terminal and storage facility in the Shetland Islands that was officially opened by Her Majesty the Queen in 1981 to handle North Sea oil. Three large tugs built by Hall Russell of Aberdeen were based here from 1978 to handle tankers loading crude oil. These 54-tonne bollard pull tugs with conventional propulsion were named *Lyrie*, *Stanechakker* and *Swaabie* after birds native to the Shetlands and were operated by Shetland Towage Ltd. In 1983 they were joined by *Shalder* and *Tirrick*, which were completed by Ferguson Bros, Port Glasgow, and at the time were the largest Voith-Schneider tractors in service in the British Isles. Continuing the theme of local

bird names were the similar, but larger *Dunter* and *Tystie* delivered in June 1996. These too were products of the Ferguson yard and had a gross tonnage of 797. The *Tystie* is seen here at Aberdeen. She has a bollard pull of 56 tonnes ahead and her main engines are a pair of 6-cylinder Caterpillar diesels of 5760bhp driving a pair of Voith-Schneider 32 G11 225 propulsion units. She is equipped for both fire-fighting and pollution control. The *Dunter* and *Tystie* replaced the *Lyrie* and *Swaabie* at Sullom Voe, the latter being redeployed elsewhere.

(Alastair Paterson)

The first Voith-Schneider tugs in the Bristol Channel were a pair for operation by Cory Ship Towage Ltd, and were based at Cardiff. Delivered in 1979, they were named *Hallgarth* and *Holmgarth*, and were twin-unit tugs built at the yard of Scott & Sons (Bowling) Ltd whose Bowling shipyard was on the River Clyde. They were part of an order for four tugs, the other pair being destined for use at Grangemouth. The *Hallgarth* is seen sailing from Cardiff when only a few months old on 28 September 1979. She had a bollard pull of 23 tonnes and was powered by a pair of 6-cylinder Ruston diesels of 2190bhp. When new, her registered owner was Finance for Shipping (R A Napier) and she was leased to Cory.. From 1985 her managers Cory changed their title to Cory Towage Ltd, and the livery changed. During the 1990s the *Holmgarth* spent a period based at Liverpool, while the *Hallgarth* was occasionally chartered to provide cover at both Devonport and Portsmouth naval dockyards. Both the *Hallgarth* and *Holmgarth* passed to Wijsmuller Marine in 2000 and they were still based at Cardiff when Wijsmuller passed its operations to Svitzer Marine Ltd in 2001. Eventually the *Hallgarth* was sold in 2008 to Falmouth Towage Co Ltd, and began a new life at this Cornish port as *St Piran*.

(the late John Wiltshire)

The Port of London Authority's Voith-Schneider tug **Plasma** of 1965 is seen in one of the two dry docks on the south side of the Royal Albert Dock in London in October 1969. She was one of four similar tugs delivered to the PLA in 1965/66 from Richard Dunston (Hessle) Ltd, and based on a tried and tested layout already in use by the Port of Antwerp Authority since 1959. The London tugs had a single propulsion unit mounted forward of amidships, which was driven by a 16-cylinder Lister-Blackstone diesel of 1600bhp. They had a gross tonnage of 122 and an overall length of 87 feet. By 1991 the PLA sold off their last dock system at Tilbury to the Port of Tilbury. Part of this deal included two of the four Voith-Schneider tugs, **Plankton** and **Placard**, which became **Linford** and **Orsett**. The other pair, **Plasma** and **Platoon**, passed to Alexandra Towing Co Ltd, Gravesend, becoming the **Burma** and **Dhulia** respectively. After Alexandra was taken over by Howard Smith Towage Ltd in 1993, the pair transferred to Swansea in 1994, and were renamed **Langland** and **Caswell**. In 1998 they transferred to Howard Smith (Humber) Ltd, Grimsby, becoming **Lady Joan** and **Lady Theresa**.

(the late C C Beazley)

Between 1981 and 1998, McTay Marine Ltd of Bromborough on Merseyside produced a number of tugs with Voith-Schneider propulsion mainly for UK tug operators. They also completed the **Cluain Tarbh** in 1992 for the Dublin Port and Docks Board in Ireland. This was their second tug with this form of propulsion, and replaced a conventional tug at the port. The **Cluain Tarbh** had a gross tonnage of 268, a bollard pull of 36 tonnes and was capable of fire-fighting. She was joined at Dublin in 1996 by a similar size Voith tractor tug, **Deilginis**, which came from a Spanish shipyard. The port authority assumed the new name Dublin Port Company and ordered two new 50 tonne bollard pull tugs for delivery in 2010. The result was that the **Cluain Tarbh** and **Deilginis** were put up for sale, along with the earlier **Ben Eadar** (of 1973), having been replaced by the new pair of Spanish-built Voith-Schneider tractors, **Beaufort** and **Shackleton**. The **Cluain Tarbh** was sold to Gibraltar-based T P Towage for harbour service at that port and was renamed **Eliott**. She is seen as **Eliott** here at Gibraltar on 19 October 2013.

(Simon Smith)

In 1981 Alexandra Towing purchased the French-built 1430bhp Voith-Schneider tractor tug *Clairvoyant* from the Progemar Group at Dunkirk, and placed her in service at Gravesend as *Sun Swale*. Meanwhile a much larger twin-unit tug had been ordered from McTay Marine Ltd for delivery in 1982. She was of 339grt with a bollard pull of 30 tonnes and she had fire-fighting capability. The new tug was named *Sun Thames* and delivered to Alexandra Towing Co Ltd, London. She remained part of the Gravesend fleet until 2006, having been taken over by Howard Smith in 1993 and Adsteam in 1999.

She was then taken into a new low-cost subsidiary company HT - Humber Tugs Ltd, based at Hull. She was renamed *HT Sword*, and given a new livery for this role. The *HT Sword* is noted off Hull on 21 April 2007. This company eventually comprised five tugs, but after passing into the ownership of Svitzer Marine, was wound up in 2009. At this point the *HT Sword* had been renamed *Svitzer Sword*, but was sold the following year to Romanian owners Black Sea Services Srl at Constanta, and renamed *BSV Anglia*.

(Simon Smith)

The Dover Harbour Board chose to replace its two twin-screw motor tugs *Diligent* and *Dominant* (see page 30) with a pair of Voith tractors that were constructed by McTay Marine Ltd. They were delivered as *Deft* and *Dextrous* in June and July 1984 and sported yellow funnels and blue hulls. They were powered by a pair of 6-cylinder Ruston diesels developing 2672bhp and giving a useful bollard pull of 29 tonnes. At Dover their duties included general towing as well as regularly docking and undocking high-sided ferries in strong winds. With the establishment of a cruise ship terminal, the *Deft* and *Dextrous* were deemed underpowered for handling large cruise ships and were replaced in 2000. They passed to Howard Smith Towage Ltd for use at Gravesend, and were renamed *Shorne* and *Cobham* respectively. The *Cobham* is seen at work in Tilbury docks on 1 November 2003 wearing the colours of Adsteam Towage Ltd. When Adsteam passed to Svitzer Tugs Ltd in 2007, both former Dover tugs were transferred to HT - Humber Tugs Ltd (see page 58), and became *HT Scimitar* and *HT Cutlass* respectively. After a short spell based in south-east Wales, in 2013 they were transferred overseas to Svitzer (Americas) Ltd for further service in Venezuela.

(Dominic McCall)

Our next pages look at Britain's rivers and inland waterways which have provided plenty of work for tugs large and small, although in 2016 there is much less activity on our canals. The 36-mile long Manchester Ship Canal was opened in 1894 and at the time was the longest inland waterway in the world. Over the years a large number of tugs operated on the canal for ship handling and also a small fleet existed to support dredging operations. Twin-screw motor tugs first appeared in 1939 and the last examples were a quartet delivered to the Manchester Ship Canal Co between November 1974 and September 1976, and known as the V-class. Remarkably all four are still in service on the canal 40 years later. All were built by the yard of James W Cook (Wivenhoe) Ltd in Essex and are tugs of 1200bhp, powered by W H Allen diesels. By the early 1980s traffic on the canal had dropped to a point where only four tugs, the V-class, were required, and from 1989 operation of these vessels was taken over by the Carmet Tug Co Ltd. In 2016 Carmet still manage these tugs, the **M.S.C. Volant**, **M.S.C. Victory**, **M.S.C. Viking** and **M.S.C. Viceroy**, on behalf of the canal owner Peel Ports Group. Looking very smart in Carmet colours, the **M.S.C. Volant** is seen at work near Eastham on 2 May 1993. The absence of an anchor is noteworthy.

(Nigel Jones)

The **Flying Falcon** was built at the Port Glasgow yard of James Lamont. She was a single-screw tug of 213grt and completed for Clyde Shipping Co Ltd, Glasgow, in February 1968. She had a 7-cylinder two-stroke British Polar diesel of 1470bhp, driving a controllable pitch propeller and had a speed of 12$\frac{1}{2}$ knots. During the early 1970s she had been equipped as a fire-fighting tug which resulted in her mast being replaced by a tall tripod arrangement with two platforms for the fire monitors. This view of her off Greenock dates from July 1975 and clearly shows this addition. The **Flying Falcon** was sold to Marine Transport Services Ltd, Cobh, in 1985, renamed **Cathaig** and registered in Limerick. Marine Transport Services Ltd was owned by. Clyde Shipping Co Ltd. In summer 1991, **Cathaig** was sold to Tremos Maritime Inc to trade under the Honduran flag as **Demon** later changed to **Daimon**. She began her Greek career from 1992 when she was purchased by Ionian Marine Tugs Shipping Co, Piraeus, becoming **Boukou L** registered in Chalkis. It is thought she was converted to a tug/supply vessel in 1994 with no obvious visual change, and as far as is known continues to work in the Chalkis area in 2016.

(Alastair Paterson)

Glasgow-based tug operator Steel and Bennie Ltd was formed in 1877. Over the years they operated many tugs on the Clyde, taking their first new motor tugs in 1957, the **Wrestler** and **Campaigner**, which were completed by James Lamont & Co Ltd at Port Glasgow. Steel and Bennie went to three other shipyards between 1958 and 1960 for three further motor tugs before returning to Lamont once more. The **Vanguard** was delivered in April 1964 from Lamont's Castle yard, and had a gross tonnage of 224. She was described as a tug/tender, and as such she held a passenger certificate for 144 persons. For her year her design was rather dated and her main engine,

an 8-cylinder Crossley diesel, developed just 1122bhp. Steel and Bennie Ltd was taken over by R & J H Rea Ltd in 1969 and in 1970 was formed into Cory Ship Towage (Clyde) Ltd. The **Vanguard** is seen here on the Clyde looking very smart in Cory colours in July 1971. She was sold in 1980 to Rocombe Shipping Ltd and retained her Glasgow port of registry. Her subsequent history becomes a little hazy. It is thought that she passed to Panamanian-flag owners in 1983, but after this little is known about her and she was deleted from Lloyd's Register in 1996.

(Alastair Paterson)

J H Lamey Ltd of Liverpool was always an innovative tug company, and in June 1957 placed into service the first motor tug on the River Mersey. She was **John Lamey** and was a former steam tug dating from 1927. The first purpose built motor tug for Lamey was the 1088bhp **William Lamey** in 1959, which lacked a traditional funnel, this being replaced by a pair of exhaust uptakes. A larger and more powerful version of **William Lamey** was delivered in March 1964 as **J. H. Lamey** and had been completed by Cochrane & Sons Ltd at Selby. She had a grt of 216 and a German MWM diesel developing 1300bhp. Three similar tugs, **B. C. Lamey**, **Alfred Lamey** and **James Lamey**, followed

in the years 1966 to 1968 from James Lamont at Port Glasgow. The Lamey business passed to Alexandra Towing Co Ltd in 1968 and the former Lamey tugs were renamed. The **J. H. Lamey** received the traditional Alexandra name of **Hornby**. Here she is seen at work on the stern of **Adelaide Star** off Gladstone lock, Liverpool, on 22 September 1974. Sold in 1984, she passed to John McLoughlin & Son (Shipping) Ltd, Larne and was renamed **Samuel F**. She was later recorded with an owner, possibly based in Malta, for use in the fishing industry and still bearing the name **Samuel F**. She was then spotted in Cyprus as recently as 2014 carrying the name **Hornby**.

(Paul Boot)

63

On page 9 I referred to a modern pair of tractor tugs for the Leith Dock Commissioners arriving in 1967 to replace two elderly steam tugs. They were **Gunnet** and **Inchcolm**, attractive looking tugs built at Aberdeen by J Lewis & Sons Ltd. They had twin Voith-Schneider propulsion units driven by a pair of Ruston and Hornsby diesels. Passing to the Forth Ports Authority in 1968 and Forth Estuary Towage Ltd in 1982, the **Gunnet** was the first to be sold in 1991. She was purchased by Klyne Tugs (Lowestoft) Ltd and renamed **Anglianman**. In 1995 she was acquired by Cory Towage Ltd for use at Hartlepool and is seen here underway on the River Tees on 14 August 1995. She was later renamed **Ingleby Cross** but was not a popular tug with crews. She was eventually moved to the Tyne, but was quickly sold in 1998, passing to Bilberry Shipping & Stevedores Co Ltd, Waterford. She is thought to be in existence in 2016 with Fastnet Shipping Ltd, Waterford.

(Harry Cutter)

The Earle's Shipbuilding & Engineering Co Ltd was incorporated as a company in 1871 and was soon building cargo ships, ferries and trawlers at its yard in Hull. Diversification saw tugs and barges completed in the 1920s, but then orders started to dry up and the yard closed in 1932. Thames-based tug owner W H J Alexander Ltd purchased a number of steam tugs from this yard from 1909 and the **Sun XV** was the final example being delivered in October 1925. Her sisterships **Sun XI** and **Sun XII** had arrived earlier that year, and all three had triple expansion machinery and a gross tonnage of 183. The **Sun XV** was later involved in the Dunkerque evacuations of 30 May and 4 June 1940, before being requisitioned by the Ministry of War Transport and put to work in the Clyde area until 1946. In 1959 the **Sun XV** received a new larger diameter funnel which coincided with the conversion of her boiler to oil-firing. The business of W H J Alexander Ltd was merged with Ship Towage (London) Ltd on 27 January 1969 to form London Tugs Ltd, and the **Sun XV** was resold in May of that year to Scrappingco S.A. of Antwerp for breaking up. In this view we see her in the twilight of her career on the Thames in early 1969.

(the late C C Beazley)

At first glance the tiny tug **Kennet** gives the impression she is a steam-powered vessel but she has in fact always been motor. She was built in 1931 as **Kennet** for the Thames Conservancy Commissioners, London, by James Pollock Sons & Co, whose shipyard was at Faversham in Kent. She was intended for use with a dredger and maintenance barges on the upper reaches of the River Thames. At only 35 feet overall length, when built her engine was a 3-cylinder Gardner of 54bhp which was later replaced by a more powerful 4-cylinder Crossley of 72bhp. Her useful life was considered over in 1971 and she was initially sold for scrap; but she was rescued in 1973 by a private owner who then put her to work as a pleasure boat on the Thames at Windsor. The **Kennet** eventually ended up on loan to the National Waterways Museum and became active on the Gloucester and Sharpness Canal for a number of years. She attended the Saul Canal Festival in July 2006 which is where she is seen in this photograph. After her owner died, she was sold in September 2008 and moved to Sawley on the River Trent. The **Kennet** then moved over to the River Weaver and was spotted advertised for sale in March 2016.

(Andrew Wiltshire collection)

In 1971 London & Rochester Trading Co Ltd completed the pusher tug **Lashette** at its Strood yard for its own account. The tug featured a pair of Schottel propulsion units and was intended for use handling barges discharged by LASH (Lighter Aboard SHip) vessels. A second similar vessel of 157grt was constructed at the same yard, and delivered to Humphrey & Grey (Lighterage) Ltd, London, in 1974 as **Grey Lash**. She had two Schottel units that were powered by Caterpillar diesels with an output of 741bhp. In 1983 she was sold to the London & Rochester Trading Co Ltd, Rochester, where she joined the **Lashette** and she was later renamed **Shovette**. The LASH system was a short-lived operation, and the tugs eventually became redundant on the Thames. The **Lashette** was later sold to Dean's Tugs & Workboats Ltd of Hull in 1998, and she was joined three years later by the **Shovette**. John Dean operates a fleet of tugs for use on the Rivers Humber, Trent and Ouse, and the **Shovette** is seen in the Humber estuary off Hull on 30 July 2007. The Humber Bridge is in the distance. To be noted are the pusher knees at her stern dating from her earlier work with LASH barges. It was in 2007 that her original engines were replaced by a new pair of Volvo diesels, giving her a revised output of 1100bhp.

(Simon Smith)

The **Daniel Adamson** is a tug with an interesting history going back 113 years, but a tug that has a very promising future too. It began on 24 August 1903 when as **Ralph Brocklebank** she was launched by Tranmere Bay Development Co, Birkenhead, for the Shropshire Union Canal & Railway Co, Manchester. She had a gross tonnage of 173 and was a twin-screw vessel powered by a pair of compound steam reciprocating engines built by J Jones & Sons. She soon had two near sisters, the **W E Dorrington** in 1906 and **Lord Stalbridge** in 1907. In 1922 she passed to the Manchester Ship Canal Co, while in 1929 she began to take up duties as a tender tug. In 1936 she was completely refitted and rebuilt with a passenger saloon and new wheelhouse. Her name changed to **Daniel Adamson**, but she was still used for towing. She remained a coal-burner all her working life, but throughout the 1960s her duties dwindled, and she became confined to tender work mainly on special occasions. This view of the **Daniel Adamson** dates from May 1977, roughly seven years before she was finally retired. The tug was then placed on loan to the Ellesmere Port Boat Museum and gradually became derelict. In 2004 an eleventh hour bid was made to save her, and she was taken on by the Daniel Adamson Preservation Society. In the spring of 2016 her restoration was completed and she was able to steam once again. A real credit to all those involved.

(Andrew Wiltshire collection)

Our attention now turns to Scotland. There were numerous small shipyards in Scotland over the years, and many of these specialised in building tugs. The most prominent builder in Aberdeen was Alexander Hall & Co Ltd which built quite a few tugs for service in the British Isles. They included the steam tug *Cruiser* for Steel & Bennie Ltd in 1953. She was by no means a small vessel with an overall length of 122 feet. She was the last new steam tug completed for her owner and was built as a coal-burner but converted to oil-firing in 1955. After ten years' service on the Clyde, the *Cruiser* was converted to a motor tug, having a 1350bhp Crossley diesel in place of her triple expansion machinery. She then put in a further six years with Steel and Bennie before being sold in 1969 to the Ardrossan Harbour Company who renamed her *Ardneil*. In 1978 she passed to Vogel, London, before commencing a lengthy spell of service with the Carmet Tug Co Ltd, Bromborough, retaining the name *Ardneil*. Carmet eventually replaced her tall steam-outline funnel with a more modern style as we can see clearly in this view of her sailing from Newport on 28 February 1991. The *Ardneil* was sold in 1999 to Aquatec Diving Services Ltd, who registered her in Takoradi, Ghana, and renamed her *Ardniel*. She was last heard of in 2011.

(Danny Lynch)

The **Applegarth** was another fine-looking tug from the yard of Alexander Hall & Co Ltd of Aberdeen. She was the second vessel in a series of six fondly-remembered steam tugs delivered to Rea Towing Co Ltd at Liverpool between 1950 and 1954. The first was the **Aysgarth**, the final example the **Throstlegarth**. Unusually for this time they were all completed as coal-burners, but were subsequently converted to oil-fired between 1956 and 1959. The **Applegarth** sank in the Canning Dock, Liverpool, on 19 August 1954 but was soon raised and repaired. However on 13 January 1960, she was run down and sunk off Woodside landing stage on the River Mersey by the **Perthshire**, while picking up the tow. Tragically six crew members lost their lives. Later raised, the **Applegarth** was pressed back into service and continued to work for Rea Towing until her sale to Holyhead Towing Co Ltd, Beaumaris, in 1971 as **Afon Cefni**. Two years later she was sold to Greek owners Maritime Commercial Enterprises A.N. Vernicos Shipping, Piraeus, initially as **Achilles** and from 1975 as **Vernicos Christina**. She was broken up at Perama during late 1980. In this view at Liverpool, the **Applegarth** is hard at work attending to Alfred Holt's **Aeneas**.

(Eddie Jackson)

After WWII British shipyards supplied a number of harbour tugs for use in the port of Mombasa, Kenya. Kenya was a British colony until 1963, and in 1951 the twin-screw steam tug **Simba** was completed by A & J Inglis Ltd, Glasgow, and entered service with the East African Railways & Harbours Administration at Mombasa. A motor tug from the Southampton yard of J I Thornycroft & Co Ltd then entered service in 1963 as **Nguvu**. James Lamont & Co Ltd completed two large twin-screw harbour tugs in 1969 and the first of these, **Ngamia**, is seen at Greenock fitting out in June 1969. Her sister **Ndovu** was completed in December. These were fire-fighting tugs of 298grt and an overall length of 115 feet. Their engines consisted of a pair of 6-cylinder Crossley Premier diesel engines delivering 2400bhp. By the late 1970s, their owners had changed to East African Harbours Corporation, and the **Ngamia** had the misfortune of sinking in June 1981 whilst moored at Mombasa. It would appear that she was never used as a tug again and was reported to have been sunk as a target by the Kenyan Navy at a later date. Her sister **Nguvu** was thought to have been scrapped in 1990.

(the late Des Harris)

The **Herbert A** was an elderly ship that did not start out as a tug. She was completed in 1911 as the coastguard tender **Watchful** for the Admiralty to be based in Newfoundland. She was from the yard of Aberdeen-based Hall, Russell & Co Ltd, which had originally established a business at the Aberdeen Iron Works in 1864. The company then opened a shipyard and built its first vessel in 1869. The **Watchful** had triple expansion machinery and an overall length of 145 feet. In 1920 she was sold to the Government of Newfoundland (Ministry of Finances & Customs) which kept her until 1927. In 1929 she underwent conversion io a trawler and was renamed **Zelda** under the United States flag. She was later sold to J Harrison & Sons Co Ltd at Owen Sound in 1936, and converted to a tug named **Northern** under Canadian registry. Between 1936 and 1969 she had a number of different names and owners, and in 1952 she was converted to a motor vessel using an old General Motors diesel engine. In 1969 she passed to Herbert Fraser & Associates of Port Colborne, Ontario, as **Herbert A**. This is how we see her at Sorel in June 1970. By the 1980s she was operating as **Tara Hall** under the Panamanian flag, but her whereabouts after 1993 are unknown.

(Marc Piché)

Your author makes no apologies for including a third splendid South African steam tug. Nineteen of the large steam tugs that operated for South African Railways were built on the Clyde. Of these, though, just two were completed by A & J Inglis Ltd, Glasgow. These were *T. H. Watermeyer* and *E. S. Steytler* both built as 620grt twin-screw vessels in 1939. The latter was launched on 23 May 1939 as *Theodor Woker* for South African Government (Railways & Harbour Administration) and completed in September. However she was immediately renamed *Stalwart* for use by the Admiralty during WWII. In 1942 she returned to the Railways & Harbour Administration, became *E. S. Steytler* and was based at Durban. She was always a coal-fired tug. Her machinery consisted of two triple expansion engines manufactured by Lobnitz & Co Ltd with a total output of 3200ihp. In 1947 she was struck by the propeller of the troopship *Georgic* and had to be beached nearby. Once repaired, in 1948 she transferred to East London, where she spent most of her working life. She is seen here in the entrance channel at East London. The *E. S. Steytler* was eventually withdrawn from service in July 1980 and broken up locally during 1981.

(the late Pernell Mizen, courtesy Trevor Jones collection)

The Manchester Ship Canal Co updated its ship handling fleet in the years 1948 to 1953 when they took delivery of eight twin-screw motor tugs from the shipyard Henry Robb Ltd at Leith. These vessels had a gross tonnage of 154 and each was powered by a pair of 4-cylinder Crossley Bros diesels of 1200bhp, which gave them a speed of 11½ knots. The first pair was **M.S.C. Onset** and **M.S.C. Onward**, both completed in 1948. They served on the canal until 1973 and 1975 respectively. The **M.S.C. Onset** passed to Holyhead Towing Co Ltd, Holyhead, in 1973 as **Afon Wen**. She is seen here as the **Afon Wen** in the Roath passage, Cardiff, on 20 September 1974. She changed hands in 1976 becoming **Kocabas** under the Panamanian flag, and received a new pair of 12-cylinder vee-type Detroit diesels in 1980. With an impressive power output of 2500bhp she passed to Turkish owners by the late 1980s. It is not sure how long she remained in use as a tug, but was renamed **Kocabas I** in 1990 for Sezai Turkes Feyzai Akkaya Construction Co, of Istanbul. She did not go for recycling until 2015 when she arrived at Aliaga.

(the late John Wiltshire)

This fascinating scene was taken in the naval dockyard during a Portsmouth Navy Day on 24 August 1975, and depicts two of the Director class diesel-electric paddle tugs. Seven of these formidable and extremely manoeuvrable vessels were built on the Clyde between 1956 and 1958, and were intended for use at naval dockyards. They had hinged masts which could be lowered for working under the overhanging deck of aircraft carriers. Nearest the camera we see the **Forceful** (A86) of 1957 and built by Yarrows Shipbuilders, Glasgow. Moored alongside her is **Griper** (A91) of 1958, one of two from the yard of William Simons & Company at Renfrew. These paddle tugs were equipped for fire-fighting and salvage and had a generous complement of 22 men. All had been taken out of service by the end of 1979, the **Griper** being towed away in February 1980 to shipbreakers at Gijon in northern Spain. The **Forceful** was sent to Pembroke Dock in 1981 for use as a target vessel at Aberporth. She was never sunk and was eventually sold to a shipbreaker at Sittingbourne. By then in a derelict state she was the subject of two failed preservation attempts. In 1990 the **Forceful** met her end in the hands of shipbreakers at Cairnryan.

(the late C C Beazley)

Of similar design to the four new tugs built for Milford Haven (page 39), were a pair for the Clyde fleet. These were built by Ailsa Shipbuilding Co Ltd, of Troon, being the first vessels to be built in the new covered building hall at this yard. The first tug delivered was *Brigadier* which was completed in November 1976 and was equipped for fire-fighting. The second tug was *Strongbow* which arrived in February 1977, both vessels being owned by Rea Towing Co Ltd and operated by Cory Ship Towage Ltd. The *Strongbow* had a bollard pull of 49 tonnes and her main engine was a 16-cylinder vee Ruston Paxman of 3520bhp, driving a controllable pitch propeller in a steerable Kort nozzle. She is seen here at Greenock in the spring of 1981. Her career with Cory was rather brief as she was sold in 1982 to Kenya Ports Authority for service at Mombasa, where she was equipped for fire-fighting and given the name *Kiboko*. Little more was heard of her for some years, but we do know that she was sold by KPA to Alba Petroleum Ltd, Mombasa, in 2004, re-gaining her original name *Strongbow*. She then became *Rhino* in 2005, before passing to Kenya Marine Contractors (EPZ) Ltd as *KMC Rhino*. As such she was reported to be involved with deep sea towage and registered in Zanzibar.

(Alastair Paterson)

The Dundee Harbour Trustees kept two tugs at the port, and it is thought that when the steam tug *Harecraig II* arrived at Dundee in 1963 she replaced the earlier steam tug *Harecraig* of 1936. The *Harecraig II* was purchased from Clyde Shipping Co Ltd in whose fleet she had been *Flying Buzzard*. She was completed in August 1951 as a tug/tender by Ferguson Bros (Port Glasgow) Ltd and she was powered by a 1217ihp compound steam reciprocating engine which gave her a speed of 11 knots. When three months old she was in collision with a tanker and sank, but was soon raised and put back into service. After her sale to Dundee in 1963 she put in 13 years' service until

replaced by the former Clyde Shipping Co Ltd motor tug *Flying Duck* in 1976. In this undated view the *Harecraig II* is seen in drydock at Dundee. She was sold to A C Cranes Ltd, of Dublin, in 1976 and by 1983 was sold and went on loan to the Maryport Steamship Museum in Cumbria, reverting to *Flying Buzzard*. The museum closed, and with a new owner, her boiler and steam engine were eventually removed. By 2005 *Flying Buzzard* had received a used diesel engine, and was now owned by Mike Nelder and Julie Jessop. They sailed her to the Caribbean as a working houseboat.

(Alastair Paterson)

Saving a ship for preservation is a massive undertaking and over the last four decades a number of British tugs have been rescued. Sadly, but inevitably, many of these projects have failed. On the other hand, the story of the steam tug **Kerne** has been one of good fortune most probably because she is a relatively small vessel and has had a lot of dedicated supporters over the years. She was built in 1913 by Montrose Shipbuilding Co Ltd at Montrose. Launched as **Viking** for a London owner, she entered service with the Admiralty at Chatham as **Terrier**. In 1948 she was sold locally to J P Knight for whom she became **Kerne**. She was then resold in 1949 to Liverpool Lighterage Co, and moved to the Mersey area. Here she operated on the River Mersey, Manchester Ship Canal and Weaver Navigation. The **Kerne** fulfilled this role until withdrawal in 1971, whereupon she was laid up in Liverpool. She later passed into the hands of the North West Steamship Co Ltd who undertook to restore and operate the **Kerne**. Her early days in preservation are recorded in this view of her passing Woodside ferry terminal 3 October 1976. Nowadays she is quite a celebrity having appeared at various maritime events and festivals as well as making appearances on TV. She survives as a fine example of a working steam ship that has served in two world wars, and is usually based at either the Merseyside Maritime Museum at Liverpool or the Boat Museum at Ellesmere Port.

(Paul Boot)

We conclude with the last generation of British built tugs By the mid-1990s, the construction of ship handling tugs in the UK had more or less ceased. The prolific shipyards of Richard Dunston (Hessle) Ltd and Richards (Shipbuilders) Ltd had ceased to build ships by the early 1990s. McTay Marine Ltd built many tugs but over a relatively short period from 1980 to 1998. One of their early completions was *Eldergarth*, a tug of 352grt. She was launched on 3 July 1981 for S J Murphy & Co Ltd (Rea Towing Co Ltd), and registered in Westport. Her sister ship *Rowangarth* was completed later the same year. After a brief spell at Liverpool the *Eldergarth* was sent out to Angola, south-west Africa for a contract at the Malongo Terminal at Cabinda. Both tugs featured the Niigata Z-drive system comprising twin stern-mounted azimuthing propulsion units resulting in a bollard pull of 42 tonnes. The *Eldergarth* is seen here at Liverpool in February 1989 when owned by Irish Tugs Ltd (Cory Towage Ltd) and registered in Liverpool. In 1999 she transferred to Shannon Tugs Ltd, Limerick, in 1999 and was renamed *Shannon*. In 2000 she was taken over by Svitzer Marine Ltd and was soon at work in the Bristol Channel. During 2009 she was sold and converted into a multi-purpose support vessel by Emut Ltd, Southampton, and by 2012 was with SafeSTS, Diss, as *Safe Supporter I*.

(Bernard McCall)

The **Point Halifax** was a significant addition to the fleet of Eastern Canada Towing Co Ltd at Halifax, Nova Scotia. She was a state of the art tug and her power output was more than double that of any existing tug in the fleet. She arrived at Halifax on 21 December 1986 after completing her trials in the UK. She was officially described as an anchor-handling tug and had been built by McTay Marine Ltd. The **Point Halifax** had a gross tonnage of 457 and a bollard pull of 62 tonnes and apparently was not a particularly good sea boat. She was powered by two 6-cylinder Ruston diesels developing 5300bhp and driving a pair of stern-mounted Ulstein azimuthing propulsion units. During her first year in service the **Point Halifax** is recorded on film in a superb wintry setting on 27 November 1987. In 1990 Smit International's 50% interest in Eastern Canada Towing Ltd was purchased by Cory Towage Ltd, and a revised livery was introduced for the fleet at Halifax. From 2001 and under the ownership of Svitzer, the **Point Halifax** occasionally worked away from her home port of Halifax, and was eventually chartered to Atlantic Towing for barge work. In 2012 she was sold to McKeil Work Boats Ltd of Hamilton, Ontario, and took the new name of **Leonard M**.

(Andrew Wiltshire collection)

Multraship B.V. at Terneuzen purchased the two former Red Funnel tugs *Gatcombe* and *Vecta* in 1997 and 1999 (page 38). When the former Red Funnel tug *Hamtun* was made available by Adsteam in 2006, this too passed to Multraship B.V. as *Multratug 16*. As such, she is seen at Terneuzen on 16 June 2008. On 24 June 1985, Red Funnel took delivery of the twin-schottel tractor tug *Hamtun* from McTay Marine Ltd. She was powered by two Stork Werkspoor (Kromhout) diesels of 2700bhp giving her a bollard pull of 35 tonnes. She was joined by her sister ship *Sir Bevois* on 8 September in the same year. In 1989 the Red Funnel Group was acquired by Associated British Ports Holdings plc, and in 2001 was resold to J P Morgan Partners Inc. In 2002 the Red Funnel Towage side of the business passed to Adsteam (UK) Ltd which had also taken control of the Howard Smith tugs operating at Southampton. The *Sir Bevois* survived the sale of her sister ship in 2006 and went on to become *Svitzer Bevois* in 2007 for Svitzer Marine Ltd, and as such moved to the Bristol Channel, being eventually sold in 2014.

(Simon Smith)

Built to replace the Director class paddle tugs (page 72) and the Confiance class, the nine members of the Adept class twin-unit Voith-Schneider tractors were completed by Richard Dunston (Hessle) Ltd, Hessle between 1980 and 1986. These were large vessels intended for both dockyard duties and coastal towing, and were designed to be used for fire-fighting and salvage operations. They had a bollard pull of around 29 tonnes and a speed of 12 knots. The **Bustler** which was allocated pennant number A225 was new in 1981, and was delivered to the Royal Maritime Auxiliary Service at Portsmouth. Here she joined **Adept**, which later moved to Portland when the similar **Powerful**

arrived at Portsmouth in 1985. The rest of the class were based at Devonport, Rosyth and Gibraltar. The **Bustler** is seen later on in her active naval career, underway in Portsmouth Harbour in June 2005. She had been managed by Serco Denholm Marine Services Ltd since 2003 and was renamed **SD Bustler** in 2008 when the former RMAS tugs were sold to SD Marine Services Ltd, Greenock. She was withdrawn in 2011 and eventually sold to Marine Salvage, Marchwood in 2013. By 2015 she had been renamed **TC Bustler** and was operating in West Africa under the Cameroon flag. In 2016 five of this class of nine remain in service with SD Marine Services Ltd.

(Bernard McCall)

Itchen Marine Towage Ltd of Southampton is believed to have purchased their first vessel back in 1969, the lighterage tug **Testgarth** of 1937. By the early 1980s a small fleet of modern tugs was gradually established, based on the River Itchen and used for local towing and contract work. Over the years two former TID tugs and a number of former RMAS Girl-class tugs were acquired, and the largest tug to join the fleet was Dog-class **Labrador**, which became **Wyepress** until her sale in 1998. Itchen Marine planned to have a new tug built in the Netherlands, but as it turned out the order was placed with the Hepworth Shipyard Ltd at Paull in Hull, the first tug built at this yard. She was launched in 1993 and delivered to her new owner in 1994 as **Wyeforce**. She was a conventional twin-screw tug of 57gross tons and an overall length of 63 feet. She had a pair of 12-cylinder Caterpillar 3412 diesels of 1348bhp which gave her a speed of 11 knots and bollard pull of 19 tonnes. Her four-bladed fixed-pitch propellers were located in fixed Kort nozzles. She is seen here at Southampton on 2 May 1997 and is still in service with Itchen Marine in 2016. The heavy use of tyre fenders is noteworthy.

(Harry Cutter)

The North British Maritime Group ordered the anchor-handling tug **Seaman** from its Selby yard. Registered in Grimsby, she was delivered to Humber Tugs Ltd, Immingham, in February 1985. She was an impressive vessel of 527grt and an overall length of 119 feet. Her Ruston 8RK270M engines developed 5760bhp which gave a bollard pull of 75 tonnes. The **Seaman** was probably ordered a little too late in the day, and was really only suited to coastal towing and offshore work in the North Sea oilfields, being too big for use as a harbour tug. She was sold in 1990 to Italian owner Società Rimorchiatori Riuniti Porto di Genova Srl and stationed at Bari as **Genua**. In 1997 she returned to UK waters as **Lady Hammond** for West Coast Towing Co Ltd, Newport, and registered at Kingstown under the flag of Saint Vincent and the Grenadines. Here she is seen departing Swansea on 2 May 1997. She was normally engaged in coastal towing while briefly based in South Wales. She then passed to Classic Marine and was managed by Klyne Tugs (Lowestoft) Ltd, initially under the Honduran flag. In 2002 she was chartered to Al Bwardi Marine Engineering, Dubai, who later purchased her. She was still active under the United Arab Emirates flag in 2014.

(Danny Lynch)

Macduff Engineering Company had owned the shipyard at Macduff at least since WW1. In 1985 its name changed to Macduff Shipyards Limited, and steel vessels were constructed in a building shed from 1987. Specialising in trawlers and fishing boats, Macduff Ship Design Ltd dates back to 1993 and has been responsible for designing a range of vessels including many tugs up to 47m in length. It works closely with shipyards around the world who construct these designs. A joint venture between the shipyard and the design consultancy in Macduff in 2009 resulted in the **Sally McLoughlin**. She was a pusher tug / workboat being an example of a Macduff Ness 16 type, one of ten available variations of the Ness class. Macduff also advertise eight other classes of tug designs in their portfolio. The **Sally McLoughlin** was delivered to John McLoughlin & Son (Shipping) Ltd, Larne, and operates in Belfast, Belfast Lough and the port of Larne. She is capable of towing, pushing, plough-dredging, personnel transfers, survey work and pilot duties. With a length overall of 16m, the **Sally McLoughlin** has two Doosan diesels, each rated at 800bhp and driving two fixed-pitch propellers in fixed Kort nozzles. Obviously delighted with the new tug her owner took delivery of a similar tug in 2013, the **Eileen McLoughlin**.

(Alastair Paterson)